TABLE OF CONTENTS

I0427765

INTRODUCTION

There has been a gradual change in the purposing of the United States' Armed Forces over the past twenty years. Since the end of the cold war, when the purpose of a large conventional force to defeat the Soviet Union was clear, the United States military has struggled to articulate a mission in peacetime that justifies its size and cost. According to recent strategy and policy documents, the United States military is no longer only charged with winning the nation's wars, but must also win the nation's peace through global engagement and partnership building.

The building partnership capacity mission may appear as a relatively new mission set for today's military planners, but only the term is new.[1] The term building partnership capacity is not yet clearly defined in joint doctrine but is used widely throughout the United States' National Security and Defense Department documents. Former Secretary of Defense Robert Gates defined building partnership capacity succinctly as, "helping other countries defend themselves or, if necessary, fight alongside U.S. forces by providing them with equipment, training, or other forms of security assistance."[2] Additionally, the *2006 Quadrennial Defense Review Building Partnership Capacity (BPC) Execution Roadmap* defines building partnership capacity as, "targeted efforts to improve the collective capabilities and performance of the Department of Defense and its partners."[3] This definition, by itself, is too vague to provide a clear understanding of the concept of building partnership capacity. It must be taken in context

---

[1] Chapter 1 of this paper will further explore the history of the United States' support to security capacity building.

[2] Robert M. Gates, "Helping Others Defend Themselves," *Foreign Affairs* 89, no. 3 (May 2010): 2-6.

[3] U.S. Department of Defense, *QDR Execution Roadmap Building Partnership Capacity Report* (Washington DC: Department of Defense, 22 May 2006), 4.

with the rest of the *QDR Building Partnership Capacity Roadmap* which further defines the partners as other departments and agencies of the United States Government, state and local governments, allies, coalition members, host nations, multinational organizations, non-governmental organizations, and the private sector. The targeted efforts are to improve support to the following objectives: defeat of terrorist networks, defense of the U.S. homeland in depth, shaping countries' choices at strategic crossroads, countering the proliferation of weapons of mass destruction, conducting irregular warfare and stability/security operations, and enabling good governance and foreign assistance.[4]

This definition from the *QDR Building Partnership Capacity Roadmap*, along with the desired end-states as defined by Secretary Gates' definition, forms the basis for defining building partnership capacity. Restated, it can be defined as the integrated, coherent, and whole of government approach to synchronize all sources of power of the United States and its partners to achieve their collective national security objectives. For the purposes of this paper, the national security objectives will be limited to those described by Secretary Gates: partner nation self-defense and the ability to fight alongside U.S. forces by providing the necessary equipment, training, and other forms of Security Force Assistance (SFA).

Current Department of Defense guidance to each Geographic Combatant Command (GCC) is to prepare a Theater Campaign Plan (TCP) to engage nations within their respective Areas of Responsibility to build partnerships and partnership capacity to preserve peace and avoid conflict. This TCP for each GCC will be the primary plan with

---

[4] Ibid., 4.

any actual war plan being a branch or sequel of the TCP. In other words, war is a failure of the primary plan.[5]

This concept may work well in terms of strategy and planning, but the assumption that the forces required for execution will have inherent flexibility and adaptability to transition between peace and war may not be valid. The missions are entirely different and the forces required to perform each of the missions may also be very different.[6] Each individual Service is required to organize, train, and equip their forces to meet mission requirements. Services see their primary mission as deterring and defeating any and all enemies, including peer and near-peer competitors and preparing accordingly. In addition, Services may not have the required congressionally mandated authorities to fully participate in the building partnership capacity mission.

This misalignment between the Department of Defense's stated goal of preserving the peace through engagement and partnership building and the way the Services are organized, trained, and equipped to fight and win our nation's wars may translate into a schizophrenic force incapable of either mission. In reality, can the same force be expected to carry out both the conventional war fighting and partnership capacity building missions successfully?

The purpose of this thesis is to explore how the United States military should organize, train and equip their forces to better support building partnership capacity operations in support of the Geographic Combatant Commanders' (GCC) Theater Campaign Plans (TCP). As stated in the *2010 Quadrennial Defense Review*, the

---

[5] Chapter 2 further explains the Department of Defense's planning guidance on Theater Campaign Plans.

[6] Chapter 4, under *BPC is Specialized Skill* addresses the different requirements for combat and BPC forces.

Secretary of Defense's priority objective of preventing and deterring conflict requires the Services to better align organization and force structure in support of national security and military strategies to meet GCC Theater Campaign Plan requirements. As the GCC's priorities change in support of our national strategies (ends), the forces provided (means) and how they are employed (ways) should also change. The assumption that U.S. conventional combat forces can do this additional building partnership capacity mission by default and "out of hide" is not valid. If the number one priority is theater engagement and building partnerships, then that mission should be resourced appropriately, in spite of organizational resistance. As the Services prioritize budgets in this time of dwindling resources, building partnership capacity should be resourced to meet the needs of the Geographic Combatant Commanders attempting to execute this mission.

War in the foreseeable future will likely be very similar to the wars we are fighting today. All wars can be placed into two categories, regular and irregular.[7] Regular force on force, conventional warfare is not likely to occur in the next decade or two as the U.S. military has the capacity to defeat any adversary that it meets in the field, as demonstrated by the Iraq invasion of 2003. The current size and capability of a potential enemy's defense forces are not comparable and the case for near term conventional war with a peer or near peer is not strong. The major world powers that might soon be peer or near-peer competitors have nuclear weapons, making total war between these nations certain suicide for the aggressor and attacked alike. What is required, to avoid war with China for example, is not the ability to start a conventional land war in Asia, but a clear policy on nuclear deterrence as it relates to our country's

---

[7] Colin S. Gray, *Another Bloody Century: Future Warfare* (London: Wiedenfeld and Nicholson, 2005), 211.

interest. We currently have a stable, deterrent relationship with China based on "a complicated nexus of economic, political, and military factors."[8] Additionally, large conventional forces do not appear overnight. Many high-tech weapons get their justification from the prospect of a conventional war with China and the time needed to field those weapons. However, the same is true for China which would need to build and train a large conventional force that could compete in the air and sea domains. The argument that if China builds a large conventional force, the U.S. will need high-tech weapons to compete is true, but China's build up will take time, and that would give the U.S. time to respond. Therefore, the surprise of a large conventional war with a peer or near-peer is unlikely to occur in the near future.

The war our nation is most likely to face is the irregular, counterinsurgency war. Forces involved in the building partnership capacity and engagement mission will more easily make the transition to fighting a counterinsurgency, as the skill sets and force structure required for each are similar. Both missions require a highly trained force adept at building relationships and adapting to an ambiguous problem set. The force structure required is manpower intensive and does not require large, high-tech weapon systems to gain access or strike the enemy. And finally, a counterinsurgency's goal is to leave in place a legitimate government with the <u>capacity</u> to provide good governance, security, stability, justice, and economic opportunity. This is the same goal post-conflict that the building partnership capacity mission works to achieve pre-conflict. As the definition of U.S. security expands to those failing or failed nation states where threats from global terrorist organizations find refuge, the U.S. will consistently find the need to

---

[8] Congressional Research Service, *U.S. Conventional Forces and Nuclear Deterrence: A China Case Study: A Study Prepared for the U.S. Congress by the Congressional Research Service, August 11, 2006* (Washington, DC: Government Printing Office, 2006), 29.

fight this type of war, directly when required (counterinsurgency) and indirectly through proxies (building partnership capacity).

Historically, counterinsurgency warfare is relatively low-tech and requires a large presence of boots on the ground to be successful. Low-tech, however, does not mean low training.

> As America is learning in this global war on terrorism, it is one thing to topple the Taliban or Saddam Hussein with our highly lethal, highly maneuverable force, but quite another to actually transform those battered societies into something better … that sort of social transformation is an up-close-and-personal effort, requiring not just lots of boots on the ground but well-trained, well-versed, and well-motivated boots on the ground.[9]

In fact, a highly-trained force will be paramount to success in fighting a counterinsurgency war in the future. It is a much more difficult type of war ranging from support to partner nations to direct combat, both before and after major combat operations. It requires a nuanced approach and a deep understanding of the problem to separate the combatants from the non-combatants and to support partner nations to establish security, governance, and rule of law.

As the U.S. fights the current counterinsurgencies, it is true that most Soldiers, Sailors, Airmen, and Marines lament the loss of what they would call core skills or competencies. It is a widespread notion that the military has needed to shelve conventional training in order to properly adapt to the demands of the current war. However, this should not presuppose that military forces should revert completely to only those skills needed in a conventional war. Their experience and training will be needed again in the most likely counterinsurgency war of the future.

---

[9] Thomas P. M. Barnett, *The Pentagon's New Map* (New York: G. P. Putnam's Sons, 2003), 104-105.

So as the Services prioritize budgets to meet the demands of the next decade, military leaders should ask if the priorities set in the *2012 New Strategic Defense Guidance*[10] make sense. Is the U.S. accepting too much risk in the most likely future conflict (manpower intensive counterinsurgency) to prepare for the least likely, but most dangerous future conflict (war with peer nation)? In the meantime, will the U.S. be able to provide security and build the capacity of our partner nations that might avert that war? Perhaps it is time to prepare for the security environment of the 21st century rather than prepare for the war our country has faced in the past.

One important mission that aligns with the characteristics of warfare in this century is building partnership capacity. In order to better understand this mission, Chapter 1 of this paper will look at the historical trajectory of the building partnership capacity mission and how it came into being as well as current trends in how our nation fights wars. In Chapter 2, the requirements for the building partnership capacity mission will be examined beginning with the President's *National Security Strategy* and the nested strategies of the Department of Defense. The chapter will end with several examples of Theater Campaign Plans and building partnership capacity requirements. Chapter 3 will look at current Service support to the building partnership capacity mission. Chapter 4 will analyze the case for building partnership capacity and propose several recommendations on both the validity of the partnership building mission and the way it could be better accomplished in the future.

---

[10] *2012 New Strategic Defense Guidance* is the common title used to refer to President Barack Obama's *Sustaining U.S. Global Leadership: Priorities for the 21st Century Defense* published in January of 2012. It is used throughout this paper as the more recognizable title.

CHAPTER 1: HISTORICAL CONTEXT OF BUILDING PARTNERSHIP CAPACITY

Although building partnership capacity (BPC) is a relatively new term in national strategy, the idea that an ounce of prevention is worth a pound of cure, especially when it comes to war, is not a new one. Throughout American history, the United States has sought to provide for its own security by expanding into regions from which threats might emanate, usually in response to an attack. In other words, the United States' presence throughout these hostile regions reduces the threat of attack on American soil. In contrast to most nations, "Americans … have generally responded to threats—and particularly to surprise attacks—by taking the offensive, by becoming more conspicuous, by confronting, neutralizing, and if possible overwhelming the sources of danger rather than fleeing from them. Expansion, we have assumed, is the path to security."[1] Early in American history, the goal was to acquire more territory as a physical barrier to outside threats. More recently, the approach has been to increase presence and influence in unstable regions from which the current threat emanates. This path to security can be split into two main types and reflects the internal debate over how best to achieve security: the unilateral, preemptive approach with direct military action or the indirect partnership approach to build internal capacity for security. In the next sections, each of these approaches will be explored to better understand the context of the current debate.

---

[1] John Gaddis, *Surprise, Security, and the American Experience* (Cambridge, MA: Harvard University Press, 2004), 13.

The Unilateral, Preemptive, Military Approach

The unilateral, preemptive, military approach has received a lot of attention following the U.S. led invasion of Iraq in 2003, but it was not the first time the United States has pursued this policy in order to ensure national security. As the next section highlights, the United States has both successfully and unsuccessfully pursued this policy in the past and, as a result, secured large portions of what today is the United States.

Early Years

The fledgling United States sought expansion across the North American continent as a means of security. For the first 150 years of American history, this was predominately accomplished through purchase, occupation, or through the use of military force to bring security to the border areas. These conflicts were manifested in the War of 1812, the Florida incursions of 1810-1819 that led to the Spanish Cession, and the Spanish-American War of 1898-1901.[2]

War of 1812

U.S. President Thomas Jefferson is sometimes labeled as "hiding" from European aggression in the years leading up to the War of 1812 by attempting to halt the impressments of U.S. sailors through economic coercion while reducing the size of the Army and Navy.[3] However, Jefferson is also credited with supporting the idea of attacking into Canada as a means to put leverage on Great Britain. In a letter dated August, 1812, Jefferson wrote, "[t]he acquisition of Canada, this year, as far as the neighborhood of Quebec, will be a mere matter of marching, and will give us experience

---

[2] Walter Nugent, *Habits of Empire: A History of American Expansion* (New York: Vintage Books, 2009), 73-220.

[3] John Gaddis, *Surprise, Security, and the American Experience* (Cambridge, MA: Harvard University Press, 2004), 14-15.

for the attack of Halifax the next, and the final expulsion of England from the American continent."[4] Although not the primary reason for the war, the acquisition of Canada was clearly one goal of the war.

U. S. expansion into Canada did not prove as easy a task as Jefferson had thought, and certainly reinforces the idea that there are limits to military power. The U. S. did not succeed in pushing the British out of Canada, nor were they able to protect the U. S. Capitol from burning. The stain on America's prestige was great and, in response, it looked to the south and west to further expand and consolidate.

Florida Incursions 1810-1819

The Spanish Cession of 1819 followed years of turmoil and conflict between Spain and the United States. John Quincy Adams, who was the Secretary of State under President James Monroe, is largely credited with the development of the grand strategy of expansion through preemption, unilateralism, and hegemony.[5] The cession of Florida to the United States is a clear example of this approach as the 1811 U. S. Congress authorized the President to preemptively invade the Floridas if any other power attempted to do so first.[6]

Following Jackson's incursion into Florida in 1818, it was Adams that pushed for the U.S. to take advantage and lay claim to the territory because it could no longer be

---

[4] U.S. President Thomas Jefferson as quoted by Walter Nugent, *Habits of Empire: A History of American Expansion* (New York: Vintage Books, 2009), 73.

[5] John Gaddis, *Surprise, Security, and the American Experience* (Cambridge, MA: Harvard University Press, 2004), 15-16.

[6] J. Freeman Rattenbury, *Remarks on the Cession of the Floridas to the United States of America and the Neccessity of Acquiring the Island of Cuba by Great Britain, 2nd Ed.* (London, 1819), Note: Extracted from the Pamphleteer No. XXIX, For October 1819), 2-5. http://hdl.handle.net/2027/nyp.33433067332746 (accessed February 18, 2012).

kept under the control of Spain.[7] The justification for the incursion was the ungoverned

space it represented and the threat to U. S. security if occupied by another foreign power

or left as safe haven from which attacks could emanate. Although a full invasion was

never carried out due to the signing of the Adams-Onis Treaty, it laid the foundation for

further expansion and consolidation of the continent. The United States remained

focused on the goal of being a regional hegemon until consolidation was completed after

the American Civil War. The next seminal moment in American expansion was the

Spanish-American War, which took the U. S. outside of the Western Hemisphere for the

first time.

Spanish-American War 1898-1901

The Spanish-American war represents another milestone on the road to American

expansion. It signified a change not only in the way Americans saw themselves, but also

a change in the way the world viewed America.

> Before 1898, few Americans took much interest in world affairs and the country
> was seen by the powers of Europe as of little account. Since 1898, Americans
> have seen themselves and have been seen by others as the arbiters of the Earth. If
> there is an American empire, 1898 was the year it was born.[8]

The war may have only lasted four months, but it brought about major change in

the way the U. S. began to see itself in the world. It is no coincidence that just prior to

the war, then Captain Alfred Thayer Mahan had published *The Influence of Sea Power*

Upon History, 1660-1773.[9] In his book, Mahan laid out the need for overseas

possessions in order to secure naval bases. This is the key to economic power: control of

---

[7] John Gaddis, *Surprise, Security, and the American Experience* (Cambridge, MA: Harvard University Press, 2004), 17.

[8] David Frum, *Morning Edition,* "American Empire," NPR, February 8, 1998.

[9] Ivan Musicant, *Empire by Default, the Spanish-American War and the Dawn of the American Century* (New York: Henry Holt and Company, 1998), 7.

the seas.[10] It is no wonder, then, that given the opportunity following the defeat of Spain, the U. S. quickly absorbed their possessions of Cuba, Puerto Rico, Guam, and the Philippines, and therefore secured naval bases that would ensure trade across the seas. This period of expansion continued through the 20th century, but not until the invasion of Iraq in 2003, did the U.S. again overtly attack preemptively and unilaterally.

Iraq 2003

President George W. Bush would have found common ground with John Quincy Adams' unilateral, pre-emption strategy in his run up to the war in 2003.[11] It is hard to imagine this was a conscious thought, but it certainly highlights that the roots of this approach are well ingrained in the American psyche. Lest we forget, the favorable vote for war with Iraq was 77-23 in the U.S. Senate and 296-133 in the U.S. House of Representatives and passed on October 10, 2002.[12] Clearly, there was little concern for the unilateral, pre-emptive approach following the attacks of September 11, 2001.

However, as in the failed attempts to attack British-held Canada in 1812, the U.S. rediscovered the limits of military power alone. The next decade was spent attempting to rebuild Iraq while at the same time fighting a counterinsurgency. This is not to say the invasion of Iraq in 2003 was unjustified, just that the U.S. did not find itself out of step with its history in launching the attack.

However, the United States did find itself out of step with an international community, and specifically the traditional partners in Europe, that had grown

---

[10] A. T. Mahan, *The Influence of Sea Power Upon History, 1660-1773* (New York: Dover Publishing, Inc., 1987), 28.

[11] John Gaddis, *Surprise, Security, and the American Experience* (Cambridge, MA: Harvard University Press, 2004), 30.

[12] CNN, "Senate approves Iraq war resolution," (October 11, 2002) CNN, http://articles.cnn.com/2002-10-11/politics/iraq.us_1_biological-weapons-weapons-inspectors-iraq?_s=PM:ALLPOLITICS (accessed February 18, 2012).

accustomed to a United States that worked to build coalitions and seek multi-lateral legitimacy. This cost in goodwill from our traditional partners was great. "According to the Pew Global Attitudes Project, between 2002 and 2006, the percentage of people with a 'favorable opinion' of the United States fell dramatically: from 75 to 56 percent in the United Kingdom; from 63 to 39 percent in France; from 61 to 37 percent in Germany; from 61 to 43 percent in Russia …".[13] As this clearly shows, unilateral action in the 21st century may make it harder to find willing partners for future endeavors. Unless the United States is prepared to tackle all of the world's security needs alone, which surely exceeds its capacity, this cost in international goodwill needs to be taken into account when weighing military options.

The unilateral approach of military attack for the purposes of expansion and security is well documented in the first 150 years of the United States (and the last 10 years), but was replaced in the next 50 years with a more indirect approach that focused on partnerships and increasing security by internal assistance to countries on the verge of collapse. The next section explores the historical sources of this multilateral approach and offers several examples.

The Indirect Approach, Building Partner Capacity

The indirect approach for expanding security for the United States has its roots in the idealistic President Woodrow Wilson. Although he was out of lock-step with the rest of the nation, his ideas certainly influenced President Franklin Delano Roosevelt's Four Freedoms Speech and his support for the founding of the United Nations. Roosevelt succeeded in bringing the United Nations into being not only because of structural

---

[13] Philip Gordon, *Winning the Right War* (New York: Henry Holt and Company, 2007), 31.

changes from the forerunner League of Nations, but because the United States had been shocked by the Japanese attack on Pearl Harbor in 1941. World War II changed the way the United States saw the world, and the threats it faced could no longer be ignored as being oceans away. As FDR put it in his fourth inaugural address:

> Today, in this year of war, 1945, we have learned lessons—at a fearful cost—and we shall profit by them.
> We have learned that we cannot live alone, at peace; that our own well-being is dependent on the well-being of other Nations, far away. We have learned that we must live as men and not as ostriches, nor as dogs in the manger.
> We have learned to be citizens of the world, members of the human community. We have learned the simple truth, as Emerson said, that, "The only way to have a friend is to be one."
> We can gain no lasting peace if we approach it with suspicion and mistrust or with fear. We can gain it only if we proceed with the understanding and the confidence and the courage which flow from conviction.[14]

As a testament to the enduring nature and strength of concept inherent in FDR's speech, these words spoken in 1945, could be written into the *National Security Strategy* today, and not seem out of place (see Chapter 2). As the next section will show, the influence of FDR following World War II will lead the United States to pursue a clear approach of multi-lateral partnerships towards achieving security interests.

The Origin of the Indirect Approach to International Security

Building partnership capacity as a means to security began to manifest itself in American policy during and immediately following World War I. President Woodrow Wilson, in his address to the U.S. Senate in January, 1917 regarding the role of the United States in securing the peace following the war, stated, "[t]hat service is nothing less than this: to add their authority and their power to the authority and force of other

---

[14] U.S. President Franklin Roosevelt, *Fourth Inaugral Address,* (1945) http://millercenter.org/scripps/archive/speeches/detail/3337 (accessed February 21, 2012).

nations to guarantee peace and justice throughout the world."[15] From this speech, he advocated that the United States, along with other great powers, should become responsible for providing peace and security throughout the world. His vision of carrying this out through the League of Nations was never achieved, but it sets the framework for the resurgence of this idea following World War II.

Rebuilding post World War II

Following WWII, the United States set out to repair the international order and establish the framework by which countries would deal with each other. Learning from the mistakes of post-WWI, world leaders understood that building peace was as important as winning the war, otherwise, a return to conflict would be inevitable. As General George C. Marshall, the primary advocate of the European Recovery Program (ERP) and for whom the plan was named, stated:

> Left to their own resources there will be, I believe, no escape from economic distress so intense, social discontents so violent, political confusion so widespread, and hope of the future so shattered that the historic base of Western civilization, of which we are by belief and inheritance an integral part, will take on a new form in the image of the tyranny we fought to destroy in Germany. The vacuum which the war created in Western Europe will be filled by the forces of which wars are made…Durable peace requires the restoration of Western European vitality.[16]

In hindsight, this vision seems obvious, but it was not so at the time. Many people in Congress, especially the isolationist wing of the Republican Party led by Senator Robert Taft, did not see the need to "bail out" the enemy. Initial 1947 State Department estimates of getting the ERP passed into law were no better than "fifty-

---

[15] U.S. President Woodrow Wilson, *War Addresses of Woodrow Wilson (with an Introduction and Notes by author Roy Leonard)* (Boston: Ginn and Company, 1918), 4-5.
[16] Forrest C. Pogue, *George C. Marshall: Statesman* (New York: Penguin Books, 1987), 240.

fifty."[17]   However, then Secretary of State George C. Marshall was perhaps one of the

most well-respected men in America, and his personal drive and campaign for the ERP

proved to marginalize the isolationist Republicans, especially when he received the

support of John Foster Dulles from within the Republican Party. Future Secretary of

State Dulles "framed his Congressional testimony with the observation 'The United

States is today a paradise compared to most of the world. But it will be a fool's paradise

if we do not make honest, substantial efforts to help others to lift themselves out of the

morass into which they have fallen. That is enlightened self-interest.'"[18]

In the end, it was the economic argument that won approval through Congress.

Estimated costs of another war in Europe were $1.5 trillion in 1948 while the Marshall

Plan was estimated at $25 billion over ten years.[19] In addition to the avoidance cost, it

was envisioned that an economically resurgent Europe would improve the U.S. economy

by creating demand for U.S. goods. "Against the economic gains of a prosperous world

and against the vast costs of a third World War, the amounts involved are a prudent

investment for a prosperous and peaceful world."[20]

Although there continues to be debate over the value of the Marshall Plan,[21] it

represents the first well-known program that institutionalized the idea that paying for

peace is preferable to paying for war. There are differences between rebuilding a nation

---

[17] Nicolaus Mills, *Winning the Peace The Marshall Plan and America's Coming of Age as a Superpower* (Hoboken, NJ: John Wiley and Sons, Inc., 2008), 138-140.
[18] Ibid., 153.
[19] Seymour E. Harris, "Cost of the Marshall Plan to the United States", *The Journal of Finance* , Vol. 3, No. 1 (Feb., 1948), 7. http://www.jstor.org/stable/2975441 (accessed February 26, 2012).
[20] Ibid., 7.
[21] Derek Yerex, *Changing Approaches to Economic Reconstruction: Lessons Learned and Not* (Dalhousie University, Canada, 2009), 5-8. http://ezproxy6.ndu.edu/login?url=http://search.proquest.com/docview/305067017?accountid=12686. (accessed February 26, 2012).

post-war and building the capacity of a nation at risk of entering a war in terms of context, but the same logic holds true; it is preferable to pay for peace.

Powell Doctrine Applied to Building Partnership Capacity

General (Ret) Colin Powell is an interesting study in the two approaches to conflict: unilateral action and self-interest on the one hand and a multi-lateral, partnership building approach on the other. At times, he appears to support both approaches. A look at the Powell Doctrine along with his other writings as they relate to building partner capacity is illustrative of the internal debate, both within the minds of our nation's leaders and in the context of policy decisions, which continue to this day.

The Powell Doctrine would be better named the Powell-Weinberger Doctrine. Casper Weinberger, former Secretary of Defense, is the original author of the tenets of this doctrine that work to define the rationale for going to war. General (Ret) Colin Powell, during his time as National Security Advisor, Chairman of the Joint Chiefs of Staff, and as Secretary of State, often cited this rationale and espoused Weinberger's doctrine to the point it has become synonymous with him.[22] The Powell Doctrine can be summarized by the following questions on the use of military force:

> 1. Is the political objective we seek to achieve important, clearly defined and understood?
> 2. Have all other nonviolent policy means failed?
> 3. Will military force achieve the objective?
> 4. At what cost?
> 5. Have the gains and risks been analyzed?

---

[22] "Powells Doctrine, in Powells Words," *The Washington Post*, Oct 07, 2001. B.02, http://ezproxy6.ndu.edu/login?url=http://search.proquest.com/docview/409198243?accountid=12686 (accessed February 29, 2012).

6. How might the situation that we seek to alter, once it is altered by force, develop further and what might be the consequences?[23]

These tenets of the Powell Doctrine are making a resurgence of late in the press, especially as the perception of the success of the wars in Iraq and Afghanistan wax and wane, and usually as a rationale for avoiding wars of "choice". However, in General (Ret) Powell's 1992 article in Foreign Affairs from which the Powell Doctrine is most often derived, he is specifically discussing only violent force.[24] In terms of force structure, he fully expects the U.S. military to be sized and shaped to meet the full range of military operations, to include non-violent missions such as humanitarian assistance and peacekeeping operations. As a matter of fact, in describing the "new world order" of the time, he paints a very optimistic picture of a world that is transforming to democracy and free markets at an accelerating rate with U.S. leadership engaged in helping all nations achieve that transformation.[25]

More than just engaging in humanitarian and peacekeeping operations, Powell claimed the President George W. Bush administration, in 2004, was about partnerships to pursue our own enlightened self interest which he described as "democracy, development, global public health, and human rights, as well as to the prerequisite of a solid structure for global peace. These are not high-sounding decorations for our interests.

---

[23] James Armstrong, Major, USA, *From Theory to Practice: The Powell Doctrine* (Army Command and General Staff College, 2010), 126.

[24] Colin L. Powell, "U.S. Forces: Challenges Ahead," *Foreign Affairs,* Vol 71, Issue 5 (Winter 1992), http://tv3wq6ms5q.search.serialssolutions.com/?ctx_ver=Z39.88-2004&ctx_enc=info%3Aofi%2Fenc%3AUTF-8&rfr_id=info:sid/summon.serialssolutions.com&rft_val_fmt=info:ofi/fmt:kev_mtx:journal&rft.genre=article&rft.atitle=U.S.+Forces%3A+Challenges+Ahead&rft.jtitle=Foreign+Affairs&rft.au=Powell%2C+Colin+L&rft.date=1992-12-01&rft.pub=Council+on+Foreign+Relations&rft.issn=0015-7120&rft.volume=71&rft.issue=5&rft.spage=32&rft.epage=45 (accessed February 29, 2012).

[25] Ibid.

They are our interests, the purposes our power serves."[26] These interests are well represented in President Bush's *2002 National Security Strategy* which linked global prosperity to global security, including our own.[27] And as General (Ret) Colin Powell remarked upon leaving the post of Secretary of State, "[t]he United States cannot win the war on terrorism unless we confront the social and political roots of poverty."[28]

Although this link was understood prior to September 11, 2001,[29] the shock of that day truly transformed the nation's understanding that threats from failing or failed states could attack the homeland. Building partner capacity was no longer just a nice thing to do; it became an imperative for protecting American citizens.

[26] Colin L. Powell, "A Strategy of Partnerships," *Foreign Affairs* 83, no. 1 (2004): 22-34, http://ezproxy6.ndu.edu/login?url=http://search.proquest.com/docview/214293195?accountid=12686. (accessed February 29, 2012).

[27] U.S. President, *National Security Strategy* (Washington DC: Government Printing Office, September, 2002), iv-vi.

[28] Colin L. Powell, "No Country Left Behind" *Foreign Policy* (January 5, 2005), http://www.foreignpolicy.com/articles/2005/01/05/no_country_left_behind (accessed February 29, 2012).

[29] Chairman, U.S. Joint Chiefs of Staff, The National Military Strategy of the United States of America 1997, *Shape, Respond, Prepare Now -- A Military Strategy for a New* Era (Washington DC: Joint Chiefs of Staff, 1997), http://www.au.af.mil/au/awc/awcgate/nms/strategy.htm#Elements (accessed February 29, 2012).

CHAPTER 2: REQUIREMENTS FOR THE BUILDING PARTNERSHIP CAPACITY MISSION

As the last chapter demonstrated, the building partnership capacity mission is new only in name. As the mission has grown in significance and won over many at the national level as a way to reduce the likelihood of conflict, it has found its way into our national guidance for policy and strategy as well as in each GCC's plans for theater engagement. This chapter will first examine the current strategic guidance and then review two of GCC's Theater Campaign Plans as examples of the requirements for building partnership capacity.

U. S. Strategic Guidance

A review of United States policy and strategy is essential to understand the context of building partnership capacity as it relates to the national security objectives. In this section, the *2010 National Security Strategy*, the *2010 Quadrennial Defense Review*, the *2011 National Military Strategy*, and the *2012 New Strategic Defense Guidance* will be examined.

National Security Strategy

The United States' *National Security Strategy* provides the framework for engagement and capacity building as the primary means through which the security of the United States is maintained and strengthened. As we "renew American leadership" to combat the threats of the current environment, "[t]he starting point for that collective action will be our engagement with other countries."[1] First, we'll continue to engage and support our long-standing allies and friends, but then we'll work "to build deeper and more effective partnerships with other key centers of influence—including China, India, and Russia, as well as increasingly influential nations such as Brazil, South Africa, and Indonesia—so that we can cooperate on issues of bilateral and global concern, with the recognition that power, in an interconnected world, is no longer a zero sum game."[2] And finally, the U.S. will further engage emerging nations to be a "model of regional success and stability."[3] All of this engagement is toward the goal of increasing the role of partner nations for the enforcement of international law and greater responsibilities for maintaining international order.[4]

The *National Security Strategy* ties maintaining international order into our own national security. "Where governments are incapable of meeting their citizens' basic needs and fulfilling their responsibilities to provide security within their borders, the consequences are often global and may directly threaten the American people."[5] In order to invest in the capacity of strong and capable partners, the United States will foster security and reconstruction in the aftermath of conflict, pursue sustainable and responsible security systems in at-risk states, and prevent the emergence of conflict.[6] Perhaps the best summary of the United States' current strategy on building partnership security capacity in at-risk states is defined below:

> Proactively investing in stronger societies and human welfare is far more effective and efficient than responding after state collapse. The United

---

[1] U.S. President, *National Security Strategy* (Washington DC: Government Printing Office, May 2010), 3.
[2] Ibid., 3.
[3] Ibid., 3.
[4] Ibid., 4.
[5] Ibid., 26.
[6] Ibid., 26.

States must improve its capability to strengthen the security of states at risk of conflict and violence. We will undertake long-term, sustained efforts to strengthen the capacity of security forces to guarantee internal security, defend against external threats, and promote regional security and respect for human rights and the rule of law.[7]

Our current national strategy calls for the United States to both improve its capability and to commit to long-term, sustained efforts to increase security in at-risk nations. Much of this mission falls to the Department of Defense and is highlighted in the Quadrennial Defense Review of 2010.

Quadrennial Defense Review (QDR) 2010

The 2010 QDR contains the most current *National Defense Strategy* and supersedes the most recent publication of that document from June of 2008. It contains the next level down strategy from the *National Security Strategy* and translates it into action for the Department of Defense. As the previous section showed, building partner capacity is one of the cornerstones of our *National Security Strategy*. In congruence with the *National Security Strategy*, the 2010 QDR highlights one of its six key mission areas as building the security capacity of partner states along with the other mission areas of defending the United States, succeeding in counterinsurgency, stability, and counterterrorism operations, deterring and defeating aggression in anti-access environments, countering weapons of mass destruction, and operating effectively in cyberspace.[8]

---

[7] Ibid., 27.

[8] U.S. Department of Defense, *Quadrennial Defense Review Report* (Washington DC: Department of Defense, 1 February 2010), 2.

Although building partnership capacity was addressed in the 2006 QDR as an area of emphasis,[9] the 2010 update elevates this mission in importance as it calls for U.S. Forces to "continue to treat the building of partners' security capacity as an increasingly important mission."[10] Additionally, it spells out key initiatives that will support the building partnership capacity mission such as:

- Strengthen and institutionalize general purpose force capabilities for security force assistance
- Enhance linguistic, regional, and cultural ability
- Strengthen and expand capabilities for training partner aviation forces
- Strengthen capacities for ministerial-level training
- Create mechanisms to facilitate more rapid transfer of critical material
- Strengthen capacities for training regional and international security organizations[11]

One important aspect of these key initiatives is the reliance on general purpose forces for implementation. Even though "special operations forces will be able to meet some of this demand, especially in politically sensitive situations, U.S. general purpose forces will need to be engaged in these efforts as well" and that they will need "specialized training and preparation for these operations."[12] Although the QDR does not go into great detail on exactly what type of training is required or exactly how this will be accomplished, it does say that in anticipation of this growing mission, the services will add 500 personnel to "train-the-trainer" positions. Furthermore, to support this growing mission, the Air Force will expand its regionally focused contingency response groups (CRGs) and investments in ISR, light attack and mobility aircraft while the Navy will increase its green and brown water maritime capacity to further enhance the security

---

[9] U.S. Department of Defense, *Quadrennial Defense Review Report* (Washington DC: Department of Defense, 6 February 2006), 2.

[10] U.S. Department of Defense, *Quadrennial Defense Review Report* (Washington DC: Department of Defense, 1 February 2010), 26.

[11] Ibid. 28-30.

[12] Ibid. 28.

force assistance mission.[13] The services' efforts to support this mission are discussed in more detail in Chapter 3.

The National Military Strategy

The *National Military Strategy* (NMS) of the United States is the first document nested in the strategy that does not specifically mention building partnership capacity as a primary goal of the military. Even though the *National Military Strategy* weaves much of the building partnership capacity theme through much of the document, it focuses on how building partner capacity is a way to achieve other security objectives, rather than being an objective by itself. The four military objectives of the NMS includes: counter violent extremism, deter and defeat aggression, strengthen international and regional security, and shape the future force.[14] In combating violent extremism, "[w]e must continue to support and facilitate whole-of-nation approaches to countering extremism that seek and sustain regional partnerships with responsible states to erode terrorists' support and sources of legitimacy."[15] Furthermore, the NMS states the only way to defeat violent extremists in the long run is ultimately through the building partnership approach that creates the environment of security and stability where "a secure population chooses to reject extremism and violence in favor of more peaceful pursuits."[16]

Building partnership capacity is also important to the 'deter and defeat aggression' mission because it is the means through which forward presence is maintained. Both rotational and forward based force posture allows for rapid response

---

[13] Ibid. 29.

[14] Chairman, U.S. Joint Chiefs of Staff, *The National Military Strategy of the United States of America 2011, Redefining America's Military Leadership* (Washington DC: Joint Chiefs of Staff, February 8, 2011), 4.

[15] Ibid., 6.

[16] Ibid., 6.

and access to the global commons. Forward force posture is only sustainable as a result of visible partnering efforts.[17]

In order to strengthen international and regional security, the United States military will continue to work with partner nations to increase security and cooperation.[18] Although the NMS breaks the world down into regions and discusses each one individually, a common theme through every region is the need to build partner capacity for security, with a focus on nations that have large, ungoverned spaces that harbor transnational and violent extremist organizations.[19]

Even the last national military objective of shaping the future force addresses building partnership capacity. The nation's military leaders must be able to gain "trust, cooperation, and understanding from our partners in an ever-more complex and dynamic environment."[20] Acknowledging the pressures of a smaller defense budget, the NMS calls for a more adaptive and flexible Joint Force that can operate with a smaller footprint, be precise and discriminate in the application of force, and possess expertise in security force assistance.[21] This infers that U.S. forces will be smaller and more highly trained so they can adapt to any mission set across the full-spectrum of conflict.

As is apparent following through the levels of the nested national security, defense, and military strategies of the United States, there is a shift from the civilian policy makers to the military leadership. Building partnership capacity is an 'ends' in the NSS and QDR, but a 'ways' in the NMS. In other words, the NSS and QDR both describe a world in which partners contribute to regional security and provide for

---

[17] Ibid., 8.
[18] Ibid., 1-2.
[19] Ibid., 10-16.
[20] Ibid., 16.
[21] Ibid., 18.

prosperity in their own country as a worthy goal by itself. The NMS describes a world in which partner nations improve their own security as a required transaction in order to meet U.S. national security objectives.

This can be seen by the weight put on building partner capacity in the following slide from the Joint Staff J5 Joint Strategic Planning directorate (See Figure 2.1). It is listed under the national military objective of countering violent extremism. In reality, it is a theme across all the national military objectives and should not be thought of as only supporting the one objective.

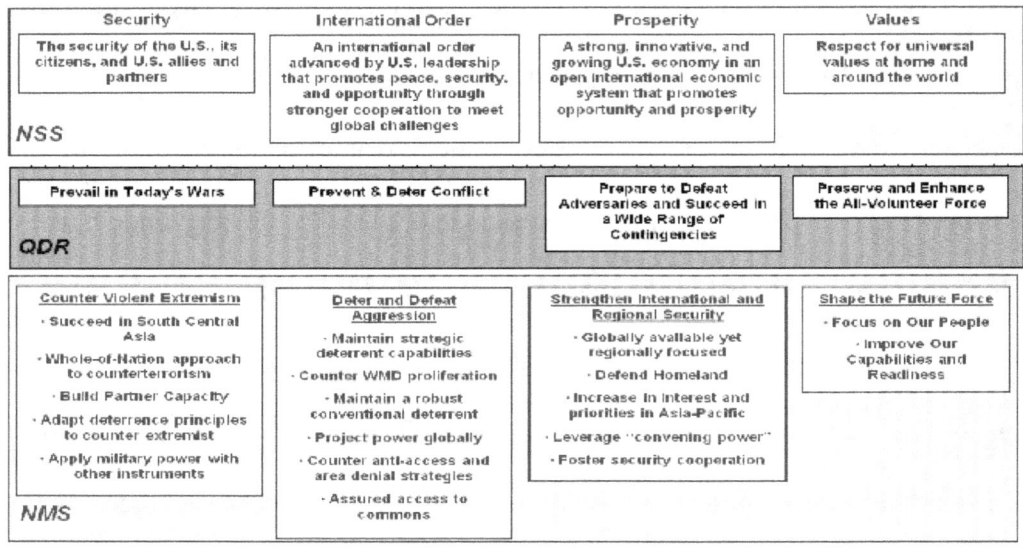

Figure 2.1—Joint Staff J5 Joint Strategic Planning Nesting of National Strategy[22]

It is, however, a good summary of how the military works to nest its strategy within the strategy of the civilian policy makers while still reframing it to meet the objectives of the U. S. military. Even though the NMS was only 6 months old at the time this slide was created, the themes of smaller budgets, a focus on the Asia-Pacific, and

[22] Roberti, John E., RDML, *Strategic Guidance and Planning,* (Presentation to the Joint Forces Staff College, 29 July 2011), Slide 5.

counter anti-access and area denial (A2AD) strategies were already under development. These themes are eventually prioritized under the *New Strategic Defense Guidance* of 2012 with building partnership capacity reduced to a lower priority than previously evidenced in the NSS, QDR, and NMS.

The New Strategic Defense Guidance 2012

The *New Strategic Defense Guidance* published in January of 2012 represents a reprioritization of the Department of Defense's efforts. Its primary shift, in light of reduced defense budgets, is toward defeating the most dangerous threat from a conventional peer or near-peer versus the threat from the most likely threat from the long, drawn-out security and stability operations such as those in Iraq and Afghanistan over the last ten years. It represents the realization that the United States cannot defeat all the threats posed by violent extremist organizations alone. President Barack Obama states, "[i]n contrast to the murderous vision of violent extremist, we are joining with allies and partners around the world to build their capacity to promote security, prosperity and human dignity."[23] Additionally, citing the example of Libya, President Obama called for more "burden sharing" by our allies and partners as a result of their increased capacity.[24] This sets the tone for the role of building partnership capacity going forward. Building partnership capacity remains important, but it will require a creative use of limited resources to meet the need. This creative use, such as exercises and rotational presence, also implies the use of traditional combat forces as evidenced below:

> Building partnership capacity elsewhere in the world also remains important for sharing the costs and responsibilities of global leadership. Across the globe we

---

[23] U.S. President, *Sustaining U.S. Global Leadership: Priorities for the 21st Century Defense* (Washington DC: Government Printing Office, January 2012), i.
[24] Ibid., i.

will seek to be the security partner of choice, pursuing new partnerships with a growing number of nations – including those in Africa and Latin America – whose interests and viewpoints are merging into a common vision of freedom, stability, and prosperity. *Whenever possible, we will develop innovative, low-cost, and small-footprint approaches to achieve our security objectives*, relying on exercises, rotational presence, and advisory capabilities.[25]

This new strategic defense guidance also lists the primary missions of the U.S. Armed Forces with "Provide a Stabilizing Presence" as number eight of ten missions the military should focus on.[26] Although this section basically restated the quote above regarding building partnership capacity, it mentioned reduced resources twice and for emphasis added, "...*with reduced resources, thoughtful choices will need to be made regarding the location and frequency of these operations.*"[27] The *New Strategic Defense Guidance* reduces the priority of building partnership capacity while at the same time highlighting the need for it to continue. While the capacity of our allies and partners is essential to the success of the new guidance, it reduces the resources put against building that capacity.

Guidance for the Employment of the Force and Joint Strategic Capabilities Plan

Before highlighting the theater's campaign plans developed to support the guidance in the strategy documents, it is important to look at the linking documents from strategy to planning. The *Guidance for the Employment of the Force* (GEF) and the *Joint Strategic Capabilities Plan* (JSCP) give additional planning guidance to theater commanders. Since 2008, the GEF and JSCP have been published simultaneously by the Secretary of Defense (GEF) and Chairman of the Joint Chiefs of Staff (JSCP) to provide

---

[25] Ibid., 3.
[26] Ibid., 4-5.
[27] Ibid., 6.

coherent direction to the combatant commanders on both the planning requirements for their command and the resources they will have available.[28]

Also, since 2008, the GEF and JSCP direct combatant commanders to develop Theater Campaign Plans that are strategy focused instead of contingency focused. This represents a major shift in the way Geographic Combatant Commands (GCCs) do planning. Instead of being solely focused on the likely contingencies as the primary planning effort, the Theater Campaign Plan (TCP) is now the primary plan with each contingency plan becoming a branch of a failed TCP.[29]

Theater Campaign Plans

The strategy-focused Theater Campaign Plan (TCP) defines the steady-state requirements to support the theater and global shaping activities. Each combatant command is responsible for developing a TCP that meets, at a minimum, the following criteria:

- A comprehensive integration of steady-state activities (security cooperation and other shaping activities) with the "Phase 0s" of combatant command deliberate plans …
- Theater posture plans as annexes to the theater campaign plans.
- Deliberate plans which become "branches" to the campaign plan.
- Identification of Supporting "force providers," that is, Services, certain FCCs, and select defense agencies and field activities, which will develop campaign support plans.[30]

---

[28] Patrick C. Sweeny, *A Primer for: Guidance for the Employment of the Force (GEF), Joint Strategic Capabilities Plan (JSCP), the Adaptive Planning and Execution (APEX) System, and Global Force Management (GFM)* (Newport, RI: The United States Naval War College Joint Military Operations Department, 29 July 2011), 2.

[29] Ibid., 9.

[30] Ibid., 7-8.

The "Phase 0" reference above relates to the joint operational planning construct where Phase 0 operations are the shaping operations to deter conflict in the beginning of a campaign plan. This interrelationship can be seen in Figure 2.2 below:

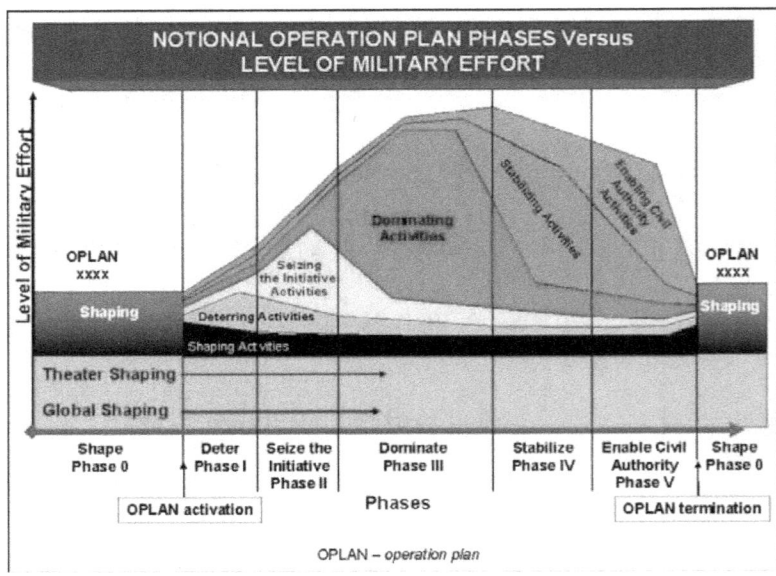

Figure 2.2—Joint Phasing Construct[31]

As global and theater shaping efforts fail to deter conflict, the branch plan is the campaign plan that follows the above phasing process (Phases 0 – 5) with a return to the steady-state theater campaign plan (Phase 0) following the termination of hostilities. Although the TCPs for each of the overseas Geographic Combatant Commands (GCCs) are classified, the following section will highlight key, unclassified components of USEUCOM and USAFRICOM TCPs from each commander's Theater Posture Statement in order to demonstrate the BPC mission demand for forces. USEUCOM's Theater Posture Statement shows the demand through sheer number of engagements in 2010 as illustrative of the requirement while USAFRICOM's Theater Posture Statement is indicative of demand by its description of the environment and approach.

---

[31] Ibid., 7.

USEUCOM Theater

The United States European Command (USEUCOM) motto is "Stronger, Together" emphasizing the synergistic strength that comes from working with capable allies and partners. USEUCOM is often characterized as being the theater with the oldest and most stable relationships and partnerships. As Admiral Stavridis stated in his 2011 Posture Statement, "[t]he most important activities and initiatives contained in these pages are those in which we work together with our allies and partners to build capacity to ensure U.S. security in the European theater and, thus, defend our homeland forward."[32] It is not without its threats, as it also contains Russia, Israel, the Balkans, Turkey, and the relatively new independent countries of the former Soviet Union. The Theater Posture Statement specifically addresses each of these threats, but rather than focus on confrontation, it looks at each of these challenges as an opportunity for "engagement and cooperation."[33]

This cooperation is perhaps best illustrated by the support from Europe to the International Security Assistance Force (ISAF) in Afghanistan. The contribution of USEUCOM to the fight in Afghanistan is best summarized below:

> Of the 49 nations besides the United States that have contributed 45,000 forces to the International Security Assistance Force, approximately 80% of them (37 nations) come from the European theater. Together, these 37 nations have contributed nearly a third of the military personnel serving in Afghanistan. And they have suffered, with hundreds killed in action. Supporting the International Security Assistance Force has given European Command the opportunity to deepen its relationships with our allies and partners, using our expertise and experience to inculcate an expeditionary mindset and train deploying partner nation forces in irregular warfare.[34]

---

[32] Admiral James Stavridis, USN, Commander USEUCOM, *House and Senate Armed Services Committees Testimony before the 112th Congress*, (2011), 1.
[33] Ibid., 36.
[34] Ibid., 36.

For many of the contributing countries in the USEUCOM region, their support of ISAF and ongoing contributions to collective security require significant training and preparation prior to deployment. Although the future requirement for training, equipping, and mentoring forces from the region for deployment is not specified, each of the service components give a detailed account of their BPC activities in 2010 and is illustrative of the ongoing requirement in the region.

In 2010, the U.S. Army in Europe trained 755 soldiers from 10 nations on Mine Resistant Ambush Protected (MRAP) drivers' training and 422 soldiers from 9 countries on how to counter improvised explosive devices. In addition, the U.S. Army taught 50 teams deploying to Afghanistan to be Operational Mentor-Liaison Teams (OMLT) and Police Mentor-Liaison Teams (POMLT) to provide 50% of the training of Afghanistan National Police and Army.[35] The U.S. Army also supported Joint and Combined Exercises, exchanged leaders with Israel in aviation, ground maneuver, training, reconnaissance, and military intelligence, and helped Romania write its tactical, operational, and strategic doctrine.[36]

The United States Navy in Europe was also busy conducting BPC in 2010. Its key effort was the Eurasia Partnership Capstone that brought in 110 sailors (senior enlisted and junior officers) from the region, including Azerbaijan, Georgia, Bulgaria, Greece, Lithuania, Malta, Poland, Romania, and the Ukraine.[37] In addition, the U.S. Navy also helped rebuild a port in Albania and contributed to several major exercises in the Baltics and the Black Sea. The focus of these exercises was on interoperability and

[35] Ibid., 16, 36.
[36] Ibid., 16.
[37] Ibid., 24.

collective maritime safety, security, and stability operations with tens of NATO and partner nations, several thousand personnel, and hundreds of ships.

In 2010, the Air Forces in Europe conducted 767 building partner capacity engagements with 39 different nations.[38] Nearly 100 of these events focused on building capacity and interoperability, especially with Poland and Romania as they developed F-16 and C-130 capabilities as well as their support operations. As a result, Romania became capable to self-deploy and sustain its forces in Afghanistan, reducing the airlift requirement for the United States.[39] In addition, Air Forces Europe trained 100 Joint Terminal Attack controllers from 15 nations to support the high-demand, low-density requirement in Afghanistan. Finally, the Air Forces in Europe participated in 60 exercises, including the validation of the NATO Response Force and supported the consortium of 12 nations' Heavy Airlift Wing (HAW) in Papa, Hungary.[40]

The USMC in Europe is the lead for the Georgia Deployment Program-ISAF and trains Georgian Infantry Battalions for deployment to the Helmand Province in Afghanistan. Through this program, the Georgian Armed Forces have significantly increased their institutional capacity to plan and conduct training for units preparing to operate in a full spectrum counter-insurgency environment."[41] Additionally, they support the USMC Black Sea Rotational Force, deploying a Special Purpose Marine Air Ground Task Force where they "conducted numerous and diverse targeted multi-national security cooperation activities with 12 partner and allied nations in the Black Sea, Balkans, and

---

[38] Ibid., 28.
[39] Ibid., 29.
[40] Ibid., 29.
[41] Ibid., 19.

Caucasus regions to enhance partner military capabilities, expand U.S. and NATO access to strategic regions, and promote regional stability."[42]

Finally, the Special Operations Forces (SOF) in Europe conducted "25 joint combined exchange training events, six bilateral training activities, 46 Partnership Development Program events, and two bilateral counter-narcoterrorism training events."[43] The Partnership Development Program was started 2007 with the purpose of training partner nations in special operations and has increased the contribution to ISAF in the area by 500%.[44] Although a very successful program by any measure, SOF in Europe laments the limited resourcing and commitment to enduring programs in SOF training.[45]

If the activity in previous years is any measure of the requirement in future years, the above service component activity indicates the strong demand for the building partnership capacity mission. In the USEUCOM region, building partnership capacity is the primary mission towards achieving its theater objectives and improves not only the collective security of the U.S.' most enduring and stable allies, but advances the ability of new partners to deploy forces in support of conflicts outside the region.

USAFRICOM Theater

The United States Africa Command (USAFRICOM) is another GCC whose "primary effort for increasing stability and deterring conflict is focused on building

---

[42] Ibid., 20.
[43] Ibid., 32.
[44] Ibid., 33.
[45] Ibid., 33.

partner capacity…"[46] As General Hamm, the commander of USAFRICOM stated in his

2011 Theater Posture Statement:

> The Command is helping African states transform their militaries into operationally capable and professional institutions that are subordinate to civilian authority, respect human rights, adhere to the rule of law, and are viewed by their citizens as servants and protectors of the people. We assist our African partners in building capacities to counter transnational threats from violent extremist organizations; to stem illicit trafficking in humans, narcotics, and weapons; to support peacekeeping operations; and to address the consequences of humanitarian disasters—whether man-made or natural—that cause loss of life and displace populations. In many instances, the positive effects we achieve are disproportionate to the modest investment in resources.[47]

With the priority of effort towards building partner capacity, USAFRICOM further

breaks down this mission into the following three parts: building operational capacity,

building institutional capacity, and developing human capital.[48] In other words, in

building partner capacity, USAFRICOM is not only improving the capability of partner

nations to address their own security concerns, but also helping them to sustain it by

ensuring their institutions have the capacity to program and budget, address their

achievable security needs, and have the people who understand these processes. This is a

tall order for USAFRICOM as demand for funding will always exceed resource

requirements.[49]

Added to the resource shortfall, USAFRICOM, for the most part, does not have a

permanent presence on the continent, although it does have several ongoing operations.

Camp Lemonnier in Djibouti has about 1,800 personnel in the Combined Joint Task

Force—Horn of Africa (CJTF-HOA) with the primary mission of enhancing partner

---

[46] General Carter Hamm, USA, Commander USAFRICOM, *House and Senate Armed Services Committees Testimony before the 112th Congress*, (5 April 2011), 3.
[47] Ibid., 3,4.
[48] Ibid., 18.
[49] Ibid., 26.

nation capacity, promoting regional security and stability, dissuading conflict, and protecting U.S. and coalition interests.[50] CJTF-HOA performs this mission "[t]hrough an indirect approach that focuses on populations, security capacity and basic human needs to counter violent extremism, CJTF-HOA operations build and call upon enduring regional partnerships to prevent conflict."[51]

Another large mission in the USAFRICOM theater is the recent deployment of approximately 100 special operations forces to central Africa to counter the Lord's Resistance Army (LRA).[52] This mission is a perfect example of how USAFRICOM is building partner capacity of the four nations combating the LRA threat: Central African Republic, Democratic Republic of the Congo, Uganda, and South Sudan. This operation is reportedly having some success. The core LRA is down to about 200 fighters according to Rear Admiral Brian Losey, commander of Special Operations Command Africa, who goes on to say, "[t]his operation is at its core what U.S. Africa Command is all about … [i]n the long run, it is the Africans who are best suited to address their regional security challenges."[53]

The final large mission is the Department of Defense contribution to the U.S. State Department led mission of Trans-Sahara Counter-Terrorism Partnership through OPERATION Enduring Freedom—Trans-Sahara (OEF-TS). Although not an enduring presence, it provides mobile training teams and Civil Military Support Elements, for

---

[50] U.S. Africa Command Combined Joint Task Force-Horn of Africa, "2012 Fact Sheet," U.S. Horn of Africa, http://www.hoa.africom.mil/pdfFiles/Fact%20Sheet.pdf (accessed February 25, 2012).

[51] Ibid.

[52] FOX News, "Obama Sends U.S. Troops to Central Africa to Aid Campaign Against Rebel Group," FOX News.com under Politics, (October 14, 2011), http://www.foxnews.com/politics/2011/10/14/obama-sends-us-troops-to-central-africa-to-aid-campaign-against-rebel-group/ (accessed February 25, 2012) .

[53] Lisa Daniel, American Forces Press Service, "U.S., African Forces Mitigate Terror Group's Impact," under "USAFRICOM media links," (February 23, 2012), http://www.africom.mil/getArticle.asp?art=7639&lang=0 (accessed February 25, 2012).

example to the countries of Niger and Mali in order to help them combat the threat from Al Qaida in the Islamic Maghreb (AQIM).[54]

In addition to these enduring missions, USAFRICOM is resourced for shorter term engagements, such as the U.S. Navy's Africa Partnership Station and the U.S. Coast Guard's African Maritime Law Enforcement Partnership to improve maritime security and interoperability. Also, in an effort to aid African countries deployed within the continent to support ongoing peacekeeping operations, such as in Somalia, USAFRICOM sponsors the African Deployment Assistance Partnership Team. Along with many efforts in logistics, military intelligence, medical, and education and training programs, the key to the success of all these programs is the ability to sustain them over the long term. General Hamm puts it best, "U.S. Africa Command maintains a long-term commitment to our partners to ensure that stability becomes self-sustaining on the continent."[55]

As the examples from these two GCCs demonstrate, the requirement for building partnership capacity efforts far exceeded the resources available in 2010. With the New Strategic Defense Guidance and reduced budgets for the foreseeable future, available resources will continue to drop with respect to the need.

---

[54] General Carter Hamm, USA, Commander USAFRICOM, *House and Senate Armed Services Committees Testimony before the 112th Congress*, (5 April 2011), 15.
    [55] Ibid., 24.

CHAPTER 3: SERVICE SUPPORT TO BUILDING PARTNERSHIP CAPACITY TODAY

As the previous chapter shows, there is a significant demand signal for building partnership capacity forces from each of the GCCs in carrying out the national strategies as illustrated by the examples from USEUCOM and USAFRICOM. In addition to the demand from each of the GCCs, DoD directed in 2009 that each of the Services prepare for stability operations by organizing, training, and equipping forces to meet the needs of the Department.[1] Although not specifically addressing the BPC mission,[2] this direction from DoD has been used by the Services as guidance in developing manuals and doctrine to support the BPC mission. The Services are responsible for providing those forces to meet the demand. Next, in this chapter, the current guidance and programs for each Service will be reviewed.

Service Specific Training and Programs

United States Army

The United States Army published an updated FM 3-07, *Stability Operations* in 2008 that revamped the way the Army looks at Building Partnership Capacity. In the preface to this document, Lt Gen William Caldwell stated, "the greatest threat to our national security comes not in the form of terrorism or ambitious powers, but from fragile

---

[1] U.S. Department of Defense, *DoD Directive 3000.05: Stability Operations*, (Washington DC: Department of Defense 16 September 2009), 12-13.

[2] There is a direct link between the types of missions conducted between BPC and Stability Operations. This is discussed further in Chapter 4. For further reading, the following reference has a good discussion: Jeffrey E. Marshall, Brig Gen, ARNG (Ret), *Skin in the Game: Partnership in Establishing and Maintaining Global Security and Stability* (Washington, DC: National Defense University Press, 2011), 32.

states either unable or unwilling to provide for the most basic needs of their people."[3] This represents a major change in focus for the U.S. Army as it begins to see the threat in a new light, and even re-characterize history to show that this has really been the mission of the U.S. Army all along. "Contrary to popular belief, the military history of the United States is one characterized by stability operations, interrupted by distinct episodes of major combat."[4]

In order to meet the demand, the U.S. Army is working to build its forces to meet the requirement. In the *2011 Army Strategic Planning Guidance*, one of the mid-term objectives (2013-2019) was to adapt the Army for BPC. Specifically, it stated, "[w]e will continue our campaign to build partner capabilities by capitalizing on opportunities to shape outcomes prior to the onset of conflict."[5] But the Army does not see this as only a mid-term objective as evidenced by the recent publication of TRADOC Pamphlet 525-8-4, *U.S. Army Concept for Building Partner Capacity, 2016-2028,* which looks to building a force in the long-term capable of performing this mission. In this pamphlet, the Army describes its core approach to building partner capacity as:

> Future Army forces apply a comprehensive approach to sustained engagement with partners to co-develop mutually beneficial capabilities and capacities to address shared global interests. Unified action is an indispensable feature of BPC. Unified action to enhance the ability of partners for security, governance, economic development, essential services, rule of law, and other critical government functions exemplify activities that build long-term partner capacity.[6]

---

[3] U.S. Department of the Army, *Stability Operations,* United States Army Field Manual No. 3-07 (Washington DC: HQ Department of the Army, October 6. 2008), Foreward.
    [4] Ibid., 1-1.
    [5] U.S. Department of the Army, *2011 Army Strategic Planning Guidance* (Washington DC: HQ Department of the Army, March 25, 2011), 9.
    [6] U.S. Department of the Army, *The U.S. Army Concept for Building Partner Capacity, 2016-2028,* TRADOC Pamphlet 525-8-4, (Washington DC: HQ Department of the Army, 22 November 2011), 17-18.

In addition to this core approach, the U.S. Army will play both a lead role in building the security capacity of partner nations and a supporting role in the areas of BPC outside its core competency, such as rule of law and economic development through five distinct lines of effort (LOE): "(1) Improve partners' individual and unit capabilities and capacity for security operations … (2) Develop partners' leaders … (3) Develop partners' sustaining institutions … (4) Foster long-term relationships that assure access … (5) Support BPC efforts led by other U.S. Government agencies."[7] The U.S. Army also sees the need for sustained effort along these LOEs and understands the need for persistence in order to realize the possible gains from this approach as outlined below:

> Proper resourcing, planning, and capability development for BPC bolsters confidence in the U.S. commitment to partners' security and regional stability. In turn, increased confidence in the U.S. commitment to partners' security and regional stability alleviates strategic gaps that enemies and adversaries might otherwise exploit, thereby strengthening the international security environment.[8]

It is important to note that in the TRADOC pamphlet, the U.S. Army considers building partnership capacity as a separate mission, not just the means towards reaching Stability Operations' objectives. This separation of the mission is not apparent in FM 3-07 which remains focused on post-conflict transition from combat operations to peace, rather than pre-conflict shaping operations. In an effort to clarify U.S. Army BPC strategy, RAND Corporation published a report in 2010 that linked the U.S. Army's guidance for stability operations to BPC as outlined in the following figure:

---

[7] Ibid., 19-21.
[8] Ibid., 24.

It is clear the U.S. Army is working to synthesize the national guidance (as outlined in the previous chapter) with current operations focused on building the capacity of nations that have just emerged from war. The tension that exists in FM 3-07 was summed up in a recent article:

> The manual predicts that conflicts in the next 10 to 25 years will not be like Iraq or Afghanistan — where the U.S. military overthrows a foreign government and attempts to create a new governing structure — but instead envisions indirect U.S. support to foreign governments that battle their own insurgencies. At the same time, the manual uses practical lessons from both wars.[10]

And finally, as the U.S. Army is planning to reduce its size, BPC is one mission area that Army leaders see growth, and perhaps future justification for the need of a large Army.

---

[10] Spencer Ackerman, "An Evolving Role for the Army," *The Washington Independent*, October 7, 2008. http://washingtonindependent.com/10768/army (accessed February 19, 2012).

United States Navy

The U.S. Navy has a long history in supporting the BPC mission and perhaps the recent change of the U.S. Navy slogan to "A Global Force for Good" was an attempt to capture that message. The U.S. Navy's *A Cooperative Strategy for 21ˢᵗ Century Seapower* was released in the fall of 2007 and represented, for the first time, a coherent strategy for the Navy, Marine Corps, and Coast Guard.[11] In this document, the U.S. Navy sets itself apart from the other services by bringing the BPC mission to the front and center of its maritime strategy. In the introduction of the document, it says, "[w]e believe that ***preventing wars is as important as winning wars***."[12] Indeed, in recognizing the tension between the skills required to meet both of those objectives, the maritime strategy rectifies the apparent dichotomy of purpose by clarifying that although the indisputable ends of seapower is to protect the homeland and defeat any adversary, the way in which the U.S. Navy will accomplish this is through building partnerships and security. Simply stated, "[o]ur challenge is to apply seapower in a manner that protects U.S. vital interests even as it promotes greater collective security, stability, and trust."[13]

As with the U.S. Army, the U.S. Navy also demonstrates a commitment to the long-term in order to carry out this strategy of building partnerships with the clear statement, "[a]lthough our forces can surge when necessary to respond to crises, *trust and cooperation cannot be surged*."[14] In order to meet this commitment, the U.S. Navy prioritizes the implementation of this strategy by fostering the Global Maritime

---

[11] U.S. Department of the Navy, *A Cooperative Strategy for 21ˢᵗ Century Seapower* (Washington DC: Department of the Navy, October, 2011), Foreward.
[12] Ibid., 4.
[13] Ibid., 4.
[14] Ibid., 11.

Partnership Initiative and training its Sailors and Marines to work with U.S. and International partners.[15]

First, the Global Maritime Partnership Initiative was designed to increase the capability to provide security in the global commons by partnering with the navies of other countries around the world. In the Naval Operations Concept 2010, this was clearly articulated as the means through which the U.S. Navy would provide Maritime Security:

> Global maritime security can only be achieved through the integration of national and regional maritime cooperation, awareness and response initiatives…The Nation's *globally distributed, mission-tailored naval forces* not only conduct the full range of related operations—from unilateral assistance at sea, law enforcement and maritime interception operations to multinational counter-piracy operations—they help willing allies and partners build the capacity, proficiency and interoperability to do the same.[16]

This initiative has its roots from 2005, when Admiral Mike Mullen, then Chief of Naval Operations stated in a 2006 op-ed, "[a] year ago, at the International Seapower Symposium in Newport, R.I., representatives from 72 countries — including 49 chiefs of navies and coast guards — discussed something called the '1,000-ship navy'…".[17] This concept was later developed in the Global Maritime Partnership Initiative that would increase security of the global maritime commons, as no single nation could produce a "1000 ship navy" alone. In concept, the idea has much merit, but may not work in reality. One of the key limiting factors in bringing the concept to fruition is the need to network navies from all countries together to perform a coherent maritime policing function. This architecture is not in place and may prove cost-prohibitive for the U.S.

---

[15] Ibid., 16-17.

[16] U.S. Department of the Navy, *Naval Operations Concept 2010, Implementing the Maritime Strategy*, (Washington DC: Department of the Navy, 2010), 36.

[17] Admiral Mike Mullen, "We can't do it alone," *Honolulu Advertiser*, October 29, 2006. http://the.honoluluadvertiser.com/article/2006/Oct/29/op/FP610290307.html (accessed February 20, 2012).

Navy to implement. "And absent the requisite technology infusion within *all* of these navies, the dream of a Global Maritime Partnership will not be realized."[18]

In addition to the Global Maritime Partnership Initiative, the U.S. Navy has developed enduring rotational partnerships in Africa and South America, called the Africa Partnership Station and the Southern Partnership Station, respectively.[19] The Africa Partnership Station (APS), for example, is a rigorously planned, thoroughly coordinated event that supports regional and country plans towards achieving measurable objectives.[20] Using these partnerships stations is the method the U.S. Navy uses to deploy forces for the desired effect of increasing regional security in the maritime domain with the desired effect of supporting the GCC's TCP.

United States Air Force

The USAF is also working to include the BPC mission into its organization as directed by the Department of Defense. In 2011, the Air Force updated its *Global Partnership Strategy* with the purpose of guiding the "Air Force on future security cooperation efforts aimed at nurturing and deepening existing partnerships and creating new ones to counter violent extremism, deter and defeat aggression, strengthen international and regional security, and shape the future force."[21] This document modified the four objectives of the National Military Strategy (NMS, see Chapter 2) into four objectives for the Air Force building partnership strategy:

---

[18] George Galdorisi and Dr. Darren Sutton, *Achieving the Global Maritime Partnership: Operational Needs and Technical Realities,* (2007), 7. http://dspace.dsto.defence.gov.au/dspace/bitstream/1947/8669/1/RUSI%2520Paper%2520Final.pdf (accessed February 20, 2012).

[19] U.S. Department of the Navy, *Naval Operations Concept 2010, Implementing the Maritime Strategy,* (Washington DC: Department of the Navy, 2010), 40.

[20] Ibid., 40.

[21] U.S. Department of the Air Force, *2011 Air Force Global Partnership Strategy* (Washington DC: Department of the Air Force), Foreward.

1.   Employ USAF security cooperation activities in support of coalition efforts to counter violent extremism.
2.   Collaborate with partner nation Air Forces to deter and defeat aggression.
3.   Strengthen international and regional security.
4.   Shape the future coalition Air Force.[22]

These objectives link the partnership strategy to the NMS and provide the ends for the partnership strategy. The methods used to achieve the desired end-states are also delineated through four key ways:

1. Establishing, sustaining, or enhancing USAF security cooperation capacity and capability.
2. Establishing, sustaining, or expanding mutually beneficial international partnerships.
3. Collaborating with partners to develop or enhance their security capacity and capabilities.
4. Collaborating with partners to develop interoperable coalition capabilities.[23]

Establishing the ends and ways is, however, only part of building a coherent strategy. The last part, determining the means becomes problematic for the document. In stating the categories of means, such as exercises, personnel exchanges, global force posture, etc., it is simply restating the ways in which this strategy will succeed by citing specific examples. In reality, the means are a repurposing of the Air Force combat forces in a BPC construct. As the *2011 Global Partnership Strategy* stated, "[w]hile continuing to organize, train, and equip our forces for combat operations, the USAF must maintain the flexibility to implement appropriate changes within our DOTMLPF[24] construct to meet our SC [Security Cooperation] ends."[25] Inherent in this statement is the assumption that forces organized, trained, and equipped for combat operations will be able to flex to

---

[22] Ibid, 7.

[23] Ibid., 16.

[24] Note: DOTMLPF is an acronym for Doctrine, Organization, Training, Materiel, Leadership, Education, Personnel, and Facilities.

[25] U.S. Department of the Air Force, *2011 Air Force Global Partnership Strategy* (Washington DC: Department of the Air Force), 17.

the BPC mission. Air Force Doctrine should certainly clarify how this should be accomplished.

In Air Force Doctrine, the BPC mission falls under what it terms Irregular Warfare (IW) with guidance published in *AFDD 3-24, Irregular Warfare*.[26] It is important to note that while the Air Force still separates warfare into *traditional* warfare and IW, it attempts to blend these two concepts by the statement, "[t]raditional warfare and IW are not mutually exclusive; both forms of warfare may be present in a given conflict."[27] Additionally, by placing BPC under the concept of irregular warfare, the Air Force is saying that BPC is a way to achieve the desired ends of irregular warfare, which are defined as legitimacy and influence over relevant population(s) through violent struggle by state and non-state actors.[28] This may limit the scope of the BPC mission in the minds of Air Force personnel to only those areas of the world where conflict is already broken out rather than fully encompassing the entire BPC mission set, such as enabling partner nations to contribute to security missions and improve security in the global commons.

---

[26] Note: Air Force Doctrine on Building Partnerships was previously its own document, AFDD 3-20, *Building Partnerships*.

[27] U.S. Department of the Air Force, *AFDD 3-24: Irregular Warfare*, Incorporating Change 1, July 28, 2011 (Washington DC: Department of the Air Force, 1 August 2007), 3.

[28] U.S. Joint Chiefs of Staff, *Department of Defense Dictionary of Military and Associated Terms*, Joint Publication 1-02, As Amended through 15 January 2012 (Washington DC: Joint Chiefs of Staf, 8 November 2010), 172.

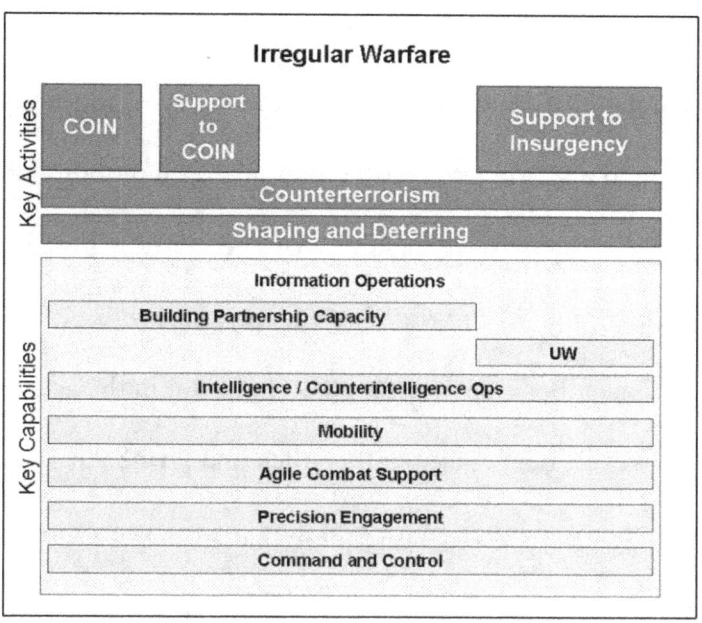

Figure 3.2 USAF Irregular Warfare Model[29]

Representing the difficulty of including BPC under Irregular Warfare, AFDD 3-24 later describes BPC as the strategy best suited to achieving success in irregular warfare, because success can only be achieved through international cooperation and commitment.[30] In the Air Force model for Irregular Warfare (see Figure 3.2), BPC is listed as a key capability.

The question then becomes, is BPC a key capability, a strategy, a support to irregular warfare, or something larger that brings the support and capability of the international community? Air Force Doctrine on building partnership capacity is at best confusing, and at worst misleading.

The concept of putting BPC forces into Air Force Contingency Response Groups (CRGs) is a good example of disconnectedness between the strategy and the means

---

[29] U.S. Department of the Air Force, *AFDD 3-24: Irregular Warfare*, Incorporating Change 1, July 28, 2011 (Washington DC: Department of the Air Force, 1 August 2007), 5.
[30] Ibid., 27.

available to accomplish that strategy. Between 2009 and 2011, Headquarters, United States Air Force (HAF) researched the need for IW, BPC, and Air Advisor requirements from each of the GCCs and found a shortage in partner nation's light mobility and air mobility systems.[31] In response, Air Force leadership developed the Air Force Concept of Employment (CONEMP) *Institutionalizing Building Partnerships into Contingency Response Forces* that added 22 new positions for each CRG (6 total in the active duty) devoted to this mission.[32] However, budgetary reality struck and "[t]he Air Force and Air Mobility Command will not have enough money, skilled manpower, or assets to meet the needs of the Combatant Commands" and will "freeze AMC's program at its initial level until possibly 2020."[33] This clearly demonstrates that even though the Air Force's *Global Partnership Strategy* supports the BPC mission, it will not budget for the specific resources, or required means, to carry it out.

Special Operations Forces

U.S. Special Operations Forces (SOF), since the early beginnings, have been involved in building partnership capacity. When United States Special Operations Command (USSOCOM) stood up in 1987, part of its charter from the Congress was to conduct Foreign Internal Defense (FID), which today is often interchanged with Security Force Assistance (SFA).[34] Special Operations Forces have eleven specific missions, three of which directly support building partnership capacity: Foreign Internal Defense,

---

[31] Colonel Konrad Klausner, *Can Air Mobility Command Meet New Building Partnershp Capacity Objectives?* (Carlisle, PA: U.S. Army War College, March 24, 2011), 5,17.

[32] U.S. Department of the Air Force, *Institutionalizing Building Partnerships into Contingency Response Force* (Washington DC: Department of the Air Force, April 2010), 16-19.

[33] Colonel Konrad Klausner, *Can Air Mobility Command Meet New Building Partnershp Capacity Objectives?* (Carlisle, PA: U.S. Army War College, March 24, 2011), 17.

[34] Congressional Research Service, *Building the Capacity of Partner States Through Security Force Assistance, United States Senate, by the Congressional Research Service, May 5, 2011* (Washington, DC: government Printing Office, 2011), 31.

Security Force Assistance, and Civil Affairs Operations. The next section will look at each one in turn.

Roles and Missions

USSOCOM is made up of each Service's contribution to the SOF mission: United States Army Special Operations Command (USASOC), Naval Special Warfare Command (NAVSPECWARCOM), and Air Force Special Operations Command (AFSOC). In addition, it has one subunified command, the Joint Special Operations Command (JSOC) responsible for establishing a joint, standing headquarters, establishing requirements, and validating tactics, techniques, and procedures.[35] Although many of the units focus on direct action missions, several key units focus on the SFA mission as their primary mission.

It is important to note that Joint doctrine still makes a distinction between FID and SFA in Special Operations publications, although these terms are used interchangeably. When referring to FID missions, the focus is on a host nation's internal defense and development "to protect against subversion, lawlessness, insurgency, terrorism, and other threats to their security, stability, and legitimacy."[36] SFA, on the other hand, is defined in the Joint doctrine as being more broadly focused supporting the capability and capacity of Foreign Security Forces (FSF) and the foreign military establishment that supports them. As the designated Department of Defense joint proponent of SFA, USSOCOM clarifies the difference between FID and SFA this way:

---

[35] Ralph Groover, Lt. Col., USA, *United States Special Operations Forces Strategic Employment*, (Carlise, PA: U.S. Army War College, May 3, 2004), 4-5.

[36] U.S. Joint Chiefs of Staff, *Special Operations*, Joint Publication 3-05 (Washington DC: Joint Chiefs of Staff, April 18, 2011), II-11.

FID and SFA are similar at the tactical level where advisory skills are applicable to both. At operational and strategic levels, both FID and SFA focus on preparing FSF to combat lawlessness, subversion, insurgency, terrorism, and other internal threats to their security; however, SFA also prepares FSF to defend against external threats and to perform as part of an international force. Although FID and SFA are both subsets of security cooperation, neither are considered subsets of the other.[37]

The third mission set that SOF performs in support of building partnership capacity is the Civil Affairs mission. Civil Affairs provide the link to host nation or partner nation civil authorities and support civilian-military operations. Civil Affairs personnel are highly trained with functional skills to carry out the role of normally functioning civil authority. Their core tasks include: populace and resources control, foreign humanitarian assistance, nation assistance, support to civil administrations, and civil information management.[38]

Although these three missions are important to SOF, there are only a handful of organizations within USSOCOM solely dedicated to carrying them out, with the Navy and Air Force providing only limited support. NAVSPECWARCOM does not have any forces dedicated to the SFA, FID, or CA missions. The SEAL teams, special delivery vehicle teams, and special boat teams generally perform direct action missions, and if used to support SFA missions, must undergo additional, recurring training prior to deployment. AFSOC has only one organization, the 6th Special Operations Squadron (SOS), dedicated to the FID mission. This squadron has recently doubled in size to support the training of the Iraqi and Afghani Air Forces.

USASOC has the preponderance of forces dedicated to FID, SFA, and CA. It is growing in size and makes up 70% of the SOF deployed to the USCENTCOM region and

---

[37] Ibid., II-13.
[38] Ibid., II-19.

number about 26,000 personnel.[39]   There are almost 10,000 soldiers in the Civil Affairs

and Psychological Operations Command, but only about 4% are in the active

component.[40] Army Special Forces go through a long training pipeline to prepare for the

FID and SFA mission. They generally can speak multiple languages and are culturally

aware in the regions that they operate.[41] The original "Green Berets", Army Special

Forces are specifically trained to conduct to the FID and SFA missions.[42]

As this illustrates, within the Department of Defense, SOF have the training,

expertise, and lead in the building partnership capacity missions, especially in the

Defense related missions of FID and SFA. However, even within the SOF community,

the complexity of building partner capacity and the requirement for ever more integration

in the "whole of government" approach may require even more specialization within that

community to achieve lasting effects. FID and SFA are relationship based by their

nature, and require persistent presence and understanding at a native level in concert with

other diplomacy and development based organizations. This may require the

development of "SOF teams that are specialists within the art of FID and SFA; i.e. non-

kinetic and with heavy focus on civil affairs."[43]

---

[39] United States Army Special Operations Command Homepage, http://www.soc.mil/ (accessed February 29, 2012).

[40] Ralph Groover, Lt. Col., USA, *United States Special Operations Forces Strategic Employment*, (Carlise, PA: U.S. Army War College, May 3, 2004), 6.

[41] John M. Collins, "Special Operations Forces in Peacetime," *Joint Force Quarterly : JFQ*, no. 21 (1999): 57. http://ezproxy6.ndu.edu/login?url=http://search.proquest.com/docview/203604654?accountid=12686 (accessed February 29, 2012).

[42] Bennet Sacolick, "Persistent Engagement: Why Foreign Internal Defense is Important," *Special Warfare* 24, no. 3 (2011): 43 http://ezproxy6.ndu.edu/login?url=http://search.proquest.com/docview/915871222?accountid=12686 (accessed February 29, 2012).

[43] Ken Watson, "Implementing an Integrated Approach to Train SOF for the FID Mission," *2011 JSOU and NDIA SO/LIC Division Essays* (JSOU Report 11-4, July 2011), 51-52.

CHAPTER 4: ANALYSIS AND RECOMMENDATIONS

The Case for Building Partnership Capacity

Building partnership capacity is essential to countering the threat from weak or failed states. Weak, failing, or failed states no longer represent a tangential threat to the United States, but are a direct threat to our national security. "Over the course of the next several decades, conflicts are at least as likely to result from state weakness as from state strength."[1] Conflicts that result from state weakness are more likely to be insurgencies or support to trans-national terrorist organizations and often can spill over to regional conflicts.[2] "Weak states pose a 21st-century threat to which our US security demands a 21st-century response. Yet weak states remain on the periphery of American security strategy."[3]

Building partnership capacity is not simply a nice thing to do in order to demonstrate the compassion of the American people. It is not something only worthy of excess resources not required to carry out the core missions of the Department of Defense. It is essential to the success of those core missions. The United States possesses the most technologically advanced and capable military in the world, yet it was brought to a standstill in both Iraq and Afghanistan. As Secretary Gates wrote in 2009:

> The United States is unlikely to repeat another Iraq or Afghanistan—that is, forced regime change followed by nation building under fire—anytime soon. But

---

[1] U.S. Department of Defense. *Quadrennial Defense Review Report* (Washington DC: Department of Defense, 1 February 2010), 9.

[2] Jeremy M. Weinstein, John Edward Porter and Stuart E. Eizenstat, "On the Brink: Weak States and US National Security", (Washington, DC: Center for Global Development, June 8, 2004), 1,2.

[3] Stuart E. Eizenstat and John Edward Porter, "Weak States are a US Security Threat." *The Christian Science Monitor* (June 29, 2004), 09. http://ezproxy6.ndu.edu/login?url=http://search.proquest.com/docview/405678235?accountid=12686. (accessed February 24, 2012).

that does not mean it may not face similar challenges in a variety of locales. Where possible, U.S. strategy is to employ indirect approaches—primarily through building the capacity of partner governments and their security forces—to prevent festering problems from turning into crises that require costly and controversial direct military intervention. In this kind of effort, the capabilities of the United States' allies and partners may be as important as its own, and building their capacity is arguably as important as, if not more so than, the fighting the United States does itself.[4]

In essence, Secretary Gates is saying the United States must accept the limitations of military conventional force on the modern battlefield since achieving victory cannot be accomplished through military means alone. In the same way a fighter aircraft cannot effectively strike with precision without a whole host of enablers such as targeting, refueling, intelligence, and reconnaissance support, U.S. military forces cannot be effective on the modern battlefield without the support of capable partners to combat the modern asymmetric or hybrid threat that has been so prevalent in recent conflicts. In this way, building partnership capacity is not more important than the core missions of the Services, but it is an essential capability to enable the success of those core missions in the same way targeting, for example, is essential to the success of a fighter strike mission.

Building partnership capacity, especially in weak states that do not have the capacity to provide security or meet the legitimate needs of its people, is essential to countering the threat they pose to U.S. national interests. There are many reasons for investing in this up front, before a state has failed or before it has become a breeding ground for trans-national crime and terrorism: building partnership capacity is preventive in nature, it is cost effective, it prepares U.S. Forces for the most likely conflicts in the

---

[4] Robert M. Gates, "A Balanced Strategy: Reprogramming the Pentagon for New Age," *Foreign Affairs*, vol 88, no 1 (January/February 2009), http://search.proquest.com/docview/197733091 (accessed April 11, 2012).

21st Century (counterinsurgency and stability operations), it improves international relations and U.S. image, and it enables traditional force on force conflict, should it arise.

BPC is Preventative and Cost Effective

The first reason to invest in building partnership capacity is the preventive nature of the investment. War is expensive. The Iraq war cost around $700 billion in direct spending[5] with total costs approximated at $3 trillion if such things as additional Veteran's Affairs costs and interest on the borrowed money are factored into the cost equation.[6] This increased expenditure in the United States' budget added directly to the national debt and erodes the economic power of the United States. Worse than the financial cost is the cost in human lives, both the lives lost and those irretrievably damaged. A small investment up front in the form of building partner capacity that may reduce the loss of blood and capital makes sense.

War cannot be avoided in all cases nor does building partnership capacity have a role to play in all cases. For example, building partnership capacity did not have a role in Saddam Hussein's Iraq due to its illegitimate government. Iraq's government was not one to support and strengthen even if there had been access granted to foreign governments and military forces. However, the cost of the Iraq war is illustrative of the cost of a full counterinsurgency. In countries that are at risk of insurgencies while struggling to improve their democracies and rule of law, such as Nigeria for example, the cost of building the capacity of the legitimate government to deal with that insurgency will certainly be less than the cost of fighting a full-fledged counterinsurgency, should

---

[5] Randall Hoven, "Iraq: The War that Broke Us—Not", *AmericanThinker.com* (August 22, 2010), http://www.americanthinker.com/2010/08/iraq_the_war_that_broke_us_not.html (accessed February 26, 2012).

[6] Josesp E. Stiglitz and Linda J. Bilmes, *The Three Trillion Dollar War: The True Cost of the Iraq Conflict* (New York: W.W. Norton and Company, 2008), 3-17.

that develop. A graphical representation of the costs associated with delayed entry into a counterinsurgency is shown in Figure 4.1. The graph on left simply represents that the required effort to counter an insurgency rises rapidly as a function of time. The graph on the right shows several examples of the level of effort and associated costs. Using several U.S. Army programs for BPC, such as the Individual Military Education and Training (IMET), Joint Combined Exchange Training (JCET), and the Georgia Train and Equip Program (GTEP) for example, the costs associated with BPC are very small, and if they preclude a large scale conflict, well worth that cost.

Figure 4.1—Intervention Options and Conflict Examples[7]

Although avoidance costs are hard to measure, since by definition the events that would drive those increased costs do not occur, the above example is illustrative of the return on investment should preemptive partnership building avert full-scale conflict. In addition to the cost avoidance from averting larger conflicts, building partnership capacity also prepares military forces for the stability operations phase of conflict.

BPC Prepares U.S. Forces for Stability Operations

Stability operations and building partnership capacity are fundamentally alike in

tasks, even if fundamentally different in context. Where partnership building seeks to

avoid conflict, stability operations seek to mitigate the effects of conflict. However, both

seek to improve the capacity of partner nations to provide for their own security. At the

tactical level, many of the tasks performed are the same as are the forces required to

successfully execute those tasks. As Brig Gen Marshall, ARNG (Ret) wrote:

> *Phase zero* refers to nonoperational activities in many of our partner countries that
> include defense sector reform and capability- and capacity-building. There is a
> great deal of overlap between these phase zero activities and SSTR[8] activities—so
> much so that the same organizations and processes that do SSTR in an operational
> construct could potentially be used to perform phase zero activities. [9]

According to the *Department of Defense Dictionary of Military and Associated*

Terms, Stability Operations are defined as those operations "conducted outside the United

States in coordination with other instruments of national power to maintain or reestablish

a safe and secure environment, provide essential governmental services, emergency

infrastructure reconstruction, and humanitarian relief."[10] Building partnership capacity,

specifically through providing Security Force Assistance in the Department of Defense's

role, works to achieve the same ends with the exception that it is preemptive in nature

and must establish a safe and secure environment where one may not have existed before.

Forces specifically trained for the building partnership capacity mission and who

perform this mission full time are arguably better trained to perform post-conflict stability

operations. However, throughout history and recently in Iraq and Afghanistan, combat

---

[8] SSTR refers to Stability, Security, Transition, and Reconstruction.

[9] Jeffrey E. Marshall, Brig Gen, ARNG (Ret), *Skin in the Game: Partnership in Establishing and Maintaining Global Security and Stability* (Washington, DC: National Defense University Press, 2011), 32.

[10] U.S. Joint Chiefs of Staff, *Department of Defense Dictionary of Military and Associated Terms*, Joint Publication 1-02 as amended 15 January 2012 (Washington DC: Joint Chiefs of Staff, November 8, 2010), 312.

forces have generally arrived in theater unprepared to conduct stability operations even though they have often been required to perform these types of missions.

> [M]ilitary commanders have kick-started economies, governed cities, managed elections and generally performed all manner of 'non-military' nation-building tasks. They have done this not only because there was no one else to do it, but because they have understood, or learned upon arrival, that getting at the roots of instability means doing much more than stopping the immediate fighting. Moreover, they have inevitably learned to perform these tasks, not from their own institution's doctrine, education, and training, but rather on the job, leveraging the wisdom found in informal networks and through personal study.[11]

Through 2008, deploying military forces received pre-deployment training in such areas as country orientation, anti-terrorism, rules of engagement, media awareness, first aid, improvised explosive device and unexploded ordinance, land navigation, and weapons qualification. They were not required to receive training in such areas as cultural awareness, cultural sensitivity, and language training until 2008.[12] As discussed in the previous chapter, Service and SOF forces specifically designed for the building partnership capacity mission receive this training as a matter of course, and with a regional focus, would be better able to pick up the pieces and rebuild post-conflict.

BPC Improves the Image of the United States

As highlighted in Chapter 1, the cost of the perceived United States' unilateral action in Iraq in terms of international opinion was high. Building partnership capacity has the ability to improve the image of the United States "through stronger international cooperation and trust, more integrated unity of effort, and improved individual

---

[11] Janine Anne Davidson, *Learning to lift the fog of peace: The United States military in stability and reconstruction operation* (University of South Carolina, 2005), 361.

[12] U. S. Department of Defense, *Training Requirements for U.S. Ground Forces Deploying in Support of Operation Iraqi Freedom,* Inspector General Report No. D-2008-078 (Washington DC: Department of Defense, 9 April 2008), 3.

relationships that could translate into improved international attitudes."[13] This

improvement in international attitudes is valuable to the United States because it

increases soft power. Soft power is the term used to describe the ability to co-opt people

rather than coerce them, or more simply stated, "getting others to want the outcomes that

you want."[14]

Not only does this international goodwill help improve the image of the United

States in those countries targeted for building partnership capacity, but it improves the

likelihood of multilateral support in solving crisis situations. The international support

from NATO countries to the Libya crisis of 2011 is a good example of how the United

States was able to co-opt other nations to support their objectives in Libya. As *The*

Economist reported at the time, "[t]he virtue of such an approach was that America had

much to gain in a world that lived by rules. By upholding such rules itself, it could

encourage others to do so too. A multilateral approach would also lighten America's

burden at times of war."[15] Building partnership capacity contributes to the soft power of

the United States which enables this multilateral approach, improves legitimacy, and

shares the burden of maintaining world stability and order.

BPC is a Specialized Skill

Building partnership capacity requires specialized skills of its practitioners. The

assumption implied in the *2012 New Strategic Defense Guidance* that conventional,

---

[13] E. John Teichert, "The Building Partner Capacity Imperative," *DISAM Journal of International Security Assistance Management* 31.2 (August 2009): 116-125, http://search.proquest.com/docview/197766575/abstract?accountid=12686 (accessed April 12, 2012).

[14] Joseph S. Nye, *Soft Power: The Means to Success in World Politics* (New York: Public Affairs, 2004), 5.

[15] "United States: Togetherness in Libya; Lexington." *The Economist,* April 02, 2011, 30. http://ezproxy6.ndu.edu/login?url=http://search.proquest.com/docview/859771895?accountid=12686 (accessed April 13, 2012).

combat forces can be used sparingly to fulfill the requirements of the building partnership capacity mission is not valid. Experience from stability operations in Iraq and Afghanistan, the raison d'etre of combat forces, the training requirements, and the length of deployment to effectively conduct building partnership capacity missions do not support this assumption.

As evidenced by the initial performance of United States' forces in stability operations in Iraq and Afghanistan, the lack of training and clear understanding of the stability and reconstruction mission by combat forces was a clear detriment to its success. This lack of preparedness for carrying out these types of missions is illustrated by the Marines' experience in Fallujah.

> [N]one of the marines interviewed … in the Spring of 2004 felt it was part of their job to negotiate trade agreements or craft an economic development plan for a city. None of the training materials reviewed reflected the intent to prepare for such tasks. Yet, following their assault on Fallujah later that year, these were precisely the types of tasks mission commanders found themselves having to conduct.[16]

It is not surprising that the Soldier or Marine did not understand the stability and reconstruction mission as his own. "Fighting is the core competency of the soldier; he is a specialist in violence. While armed forces can serve many purposes, what defines them uniquely is their ability to damage things and injure or kill people as a legitimate instrument of the polity."[17] In other words, combat forces are trained to perform combat. Asking them to perform the additional roles of building partnership capacity, stability operations, or reconstruction efforts takes away from their core competency and limits their effectiveness at either mission.

---

[16] Janine Anne Davidson, *Learning to lift the fog of peace: The United States military in stability and reconstruction operation* (University of South Carolina, 2005), 358.
[17] Colin S. Gray, *Hard Power and Soft Power: The Utility of Military Force as an Instrument of Policy in the 21st Century* (Carlisle, PA: Strategic Studies Institute, 2011), 1.

Specialized forces are required for the building partnership capacity and stability and reconstruction missions just as specialized forces are required for combat missions. The assumption that the same military forces can perform both missions well may look good on a Pentagon balance sheet during a budget crisis, but asking the individual Soldier, Airman, Marine, or Sailor to perform both missions concurrently is another thing altogether.

In addition to the difficulty in performing two very different tasks simultaneously, it is counterproductive in terms of training. Time spent training for combat operations is time lost training for building partnership capacity and stability operations. As an example on a smaller scale, the SOF community has experience with both direct action and SFA missions and the resulting difficulty in preparing the same force for both missions. As one SOF operator lamented:

> Attempting to train our operators to be experts in both areas potentially wastes precious training resources and is counterproductive in light of the diversity of the missions. Furthermore, increasing time on station requirements in order to grow regional specialists would not coincide with the operations requirements of traditional direct action forces/teams. To attempt to mix these two distinct tracks would undermine the specialization necessary to perform both with the necessary proficiency.[18]

Additionally, these two distinct types of missions do not call for the same personnel to perform them nor are the same kinds of people attracted to them. Combat forces require generally young, unmarried males while the building partnership capacity and stability missions require older, gender-balanced, more educated forces.[19] The requirement for distinct forces to separately perform combat and building partnership capacity missions makes sense in both training and effectiveness.

---

[18] Ken Watson, "Implementing an Integrated Approach to Train SOF for the FID Mission," *2011 JSOU and NDIA SO/LIC Division Essays* (JSOU Report 11-4, July 2011), 51.

[19] Thomas P. M. Barnett, *The Pentagon's New Map* (New York: G. P. Putnam's Sons, 2003), 321.

Interagency Coordination

Although a detailed examination of the interagency coordination and planning

process is outside the scope of this paper, it is important to understand the interagency

process as it relates to building partnership capacity. For that purpose, a brief discussion

of the process and other agencies' agendas is illuminative of the Department of Defense's

role. Interagency coordination is one of the most difficult tasks confronting practitioners

of building partnership capacity. As defined earlier, building partnership capacity

requires a whole of government approach to effectively carry out the three "D's" of

foreign policy: Defense, Diplomacy, and Development. The principle departments of

government that support the three "D's" are the Department of Defense and the

Department of State along with its reporting agency, the United States Agency for

International Development (USAID). Other agencies and departments, such as the

Department of Treasury and Department of Justice, also contribute to the building

partnership capacity mission, but in a diminished role relative to the Departments of State

and Defense. Coordination across these agencies has been difficult and fraught with

bureaucratic barriers to funding, resources, and planning.

Department of State

The Department of State released its first *Quadrennial Diplomacy and*

Development Review (QDDR) in 2010. In this report, the Department of State identified

itself as the lead department for conflict prevention and stability:

> We start by embracing crisis and conflict prevention and resolution; the
> promotion of sustainable, responsible, and effective security and governance in
> fragile states; and fostering security and reconstruction in the aftermath of conflict

as a central national security objective and as a core State mission that must be closely supported by USAID and many other U.S. government agencies.[20]

This statement formally acknowledges the lead role of the State Department in conflict prevention and stability operations and formalized the coordinating authority of the Office of the Coordinator for Reconstruction and Stabilization (S/CRS). However, within the State Department, there were a myriad of other offices that supported the S/CRS' mission such as the Bureaus of Political-Military Affairs (PM), International Narcotics and Law Enforcement Affairs (INL), Population, Refugees, and Migration, along with the newly created Bureau of Counterterrorism. The QDDR, with Congressional approval, elevated the S/CRS to Bureau status, and established an Undersecretary of Civilian Security, Democracy and Human Rights to "bring together the diplomatic and operational capabilities needed to build sustainable security and justice sector capacity, protect individuals from violence, oppression, discrimination, and want in many different contexts, and promote democracy and global human rights."[21] The Bureau of Conflict and Stabilization Operations (CSO, formerly S/CRS) is still responsible for the civilian led conflict prevention and development in fragile states.

USAID is the primary agency within the State Department for development and has a sister organization to CSO called the Bureau for Democracy, Conflict, and Humanitarian Assistance (DCHA). This Bureau has several offices that support the building partnership capacity mission such as the Office of Transition Initiatives (OTI), the Conflict Mitigation and Management Office (CMM), and the Office of Foreign

---

[20] U.S. Department of State, *Quadrennial Diplomacy and Development Review—Leading Through Civilian Power* (Washington DC: Government Printing Office, 2010), 123-124.
[21] Ibid., 135.

Disaster Assistance (OFDA). These offices support "a development approach that focuses on democracy and governance as a critical frame for success."[22]

However, the Bureau of Conflict and Stabilization Operations and USAID are hardly comparable to the scale of the Defense Department's efforts and resources. For example, CSO is working only two to three large projects, certainly not on a global scale as originally envisioned.[23] In addition, the level of Congressional funding for these State Department programs is well below that of Security Assistance programs within the Department of Defense. Current 2012 funding for the Department of State (including USAID) is $32.48 billion as compared to $707.466 billion for the Department of Defense.[24] This is why former Defense Secretary Gates said:

> It has become clear that America's civilian institutions of diplomacy and development have been chronically undermanned and underfunded for far too long – relative to what we spend on the military, and more important, relative to the responsibilities and challenges our nation has around the world. I cannot pretend to know the right dollar amount – I know it's a good deal more than the one percent of the federal budget that it is right now.[25]

Even with additional resources, the Department of State and USAID would have a difficult time coordinating the whole of government approach to building partnership capacity without control of the International Assistance budget. Each government department controls its own portion of the International Assistance budget, and the majority of those monies arrive earmarked from Congress. An example of this can be seen in SFA funding authorities shown in Figure 4.2.

---

[22] Ibid., 132.

[23] U.S. Department of State, "Our Work," Bureau of Conflict and Stabilization Operations, http://www.state.gov/j/cso/ourwork/index.htm (accessed April 12, 2012).

[24] *Historical tables: Budget of the United States Government, Fiscal Year 2012* (Washington DC: U.S. Government Printing Office, 2012), 83.

[25] Robert M. Gates, Speech to the U.S. Global Leadership Campaign, July 15, 2008, http://www.defense.gov/speeches/speech.aspx?speechid=1262 (accessed April 13, 2012).

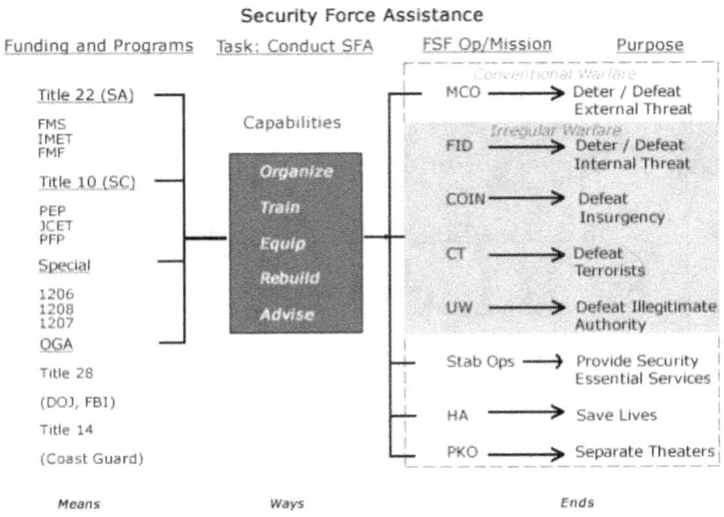

Figure 4.2 Summary of Funding Authorities for SFA[26]

Even with pooled funding, such as the Global Security Contingency Fund (GSCF)[27],

Congress has set limits on the amount of money that can be allocated to that fund and

specified missions and countries where it can be used.[28] Additionally, the set limit of

$350 million for 2012 represents only 1/2% of the total International Affairs budget of

$56.252 billion.[29] Although a good start, the GSCF makes little difference to overall

flexibility in planning and execution as the limits imposed by Congress amount to

nothing more than the same earmarked funds under a different name.

The final barrier to interagency coordination is the lack of planning capability at

the top levels of the U.S. government to effectively tackle the difficult problems of the

---

[26] Congressional Research Service, *Building the Capacity of Partner States Through Security Force Assistance, United States Senate, by the Congressional Research Service, May 5, 2011* (Washington, DC: government Printing Office, 2011), 14.

[27] Ibid., 54-57.

[28] Kate Brannen, "U.S. Defense Bill Limits DoD-State Fund," *DefenseNews.com*, December 13, 2011, http://www.defensenews.com/article/20111213/DEFSECT04/112130311/U-S-Defense-Bill-Limits-DoD-State-Fund (accessed April 13, 2012).

[29] *Historical tables: Budget of the United States Government, Fiscal Year 2012* (Washington DC: U.S. Government Printing Office, 2012), 55.

current strategic environment as characterized by rapidly changing global conditions and uncertainty. As former Undersecretary of Defense for Policy, Michele Flournoy stated:

> The reality is that America's most fundamental deliberations are made in an environment that remains dominated by the needs of the present and the cacophony of current crises. There must be a better way. Given that the United States has embarked on what is surely another long twilight struggle, it is past time to make a serious and sustained effort at integrating all the elements of national power in a manner that creates the unity of effort necessary for victory.[30]

Building partnership capacity is only one aspect of exercising national power, but it is essential that for it to be effective, decisions made on priorities and resourcing that inherently have a coercive effect on the various Departments responsible for carrying it out come from the National Security Council level of the U.S. government.

Recommendations to Improve BPC Mission Effectiveness

As this paper has shown, the Department of Defense, and each of the Services have extolled the virtues of building partnership capacity. From the President's *National Security Strategy* all the way down to the Service doctrine and through the Geographic Combatant Commander's TCPs, each document supports and directs its component or command to resource the building partnership capacity mission. But when it comes to prioritization of limited resources, building partnership capacity is the first on the chopping block. This does not remove the requirement for building partnership capacity missions nor does it eliminate the need to create specialized forces capable of effectively carrying them out with the right training and equipment.

---

[30] Michele A. Flournoy and Shawn W. Brimley, "Strategic Planning for National Security: The New Project Solarium," *Joint Forces Quarterly* 41, 2nd Quarter (2006): 81.

This does not mean the core missions of the Services are any less important or that these missions should not still receive the lion's share of the resources allocated in the Defense budget. The need for a conventional force capable of destroying any potential enemy is a fundamental requirement of U.S. national security. However, this force has limits in its ability to deal with the current threats from asymmetrical or hybrid warfare. To complement this traditional force, a much smaller, specialized building partnership capacity force is required to successfully defeat the current threats. Several options for how to create this force, in order of required change in organizational structure, are presented below.

Refine the Role of the Services

Each of the Service components of the Department of Defense have well-established core missions that support the Joint warfighting effort. In recent conflicts, where there has been a clearly defined enemy on the battlefield, the U.S. conventional forces have demonstrated the capability to rapidly defeat that enemy's conventional combat capabilities through the Joint employment of their inherent core missions. In an effort to continually improve that core mission capability, the Services have not developed sufficient specialized forces capable of meeting the demand for the building partnership capacity mission. In order to better meet the demand, the Services should support the priority of this mission by establishing new organizations with building partnership capacity as their primary mission.

There are many recommendations on how the Services could organize to better support the building partnership capacity mission. One such recommendation for the U.S. Army is to establish a Security Advisory and Assistance Command that would report to the U.S. Army Training and Doctrine Command (TRADOC).[31] This organization would bring all the training and SFA components under one command and further organize into deployable teams in the form of Military Advisory and Assistance Commands (MAACs).[32] Whether these new organizations were at the Major Command (MAJCOM) level or below would depend on the relative effort of the Service in the building partnership capacity mission. The important change such a new organization would bring is the single unity of purpose for the organization and an advocate for the mission rather than the current ad hoc approach.

It is unlikely, however, that this will happen anytime soon. In the same manner that Special Operations Forces were often shortchanged by the Services prior to the establishment of USSOCOM, the Services will continue to under-resource the building partnership capacity mission. If another event highlights this shortfall, such as the failure of the Iranian hostage rescue attempt did for SOF, then the Services may lose some of the resourcing to build an organization whose sole purpose is provide the building partnership capacity mission. One such organization that could expand its current support to building partnership capacity is USSOCOM.

Expansion of Special Operations Indirect Capabilities

Another option to ensure unity of effort and to provide a single point of contact to outside agencies and departments would be to expand the SOF capability for Security Force Assistance. As USSOCOM continues to grow its Direct Action capability, it could also continue to grow its indirect capability by further expanding its dedicated SFA

---

[31] Scott G. Wuestner, *Building Partner Capacity/Security Force Assistance: A New Structural Paradigm* (Carlisle, PA: The Strategic Studies Institute, February 2009), 38.
[32] Ibid., 41.

forces and consolidating them as a sub-unified command under USSOCOM. Component SOF units that specifically support building partnership capacity, such as the 6th SOS, currently under Air Force Special Operations Command (AFSOC), could be brought under the Building Partnership Capacity Sub-unified Command. USSOCOM would be the force provider to the GCCs to fulfill building partnership capacity requirements in their TCPs. One significant advantage of this approach is that USSOCOM already has the infrastructure in place to coordinate with the GCCs through its Theater Special Operations Commands (TSOCs) for mission execution.[33] In addition, this approach centralizes the building partnership capacity forces under a single force provider with separate funding to organize, train, and equip those forces.

Sub-unified Command at the Combatant Command

Another proposal is to establish a sub-unified command at each of the GCCs to coordinate building partnership capacity activities within their respective theaters.[34] The natural advantage of this approach is that the majority of defense planning occurs at the GCC since it represents the operational nexus between strategic guidance and tactical information. "At the theater level, the GCC provides the natural place where resources and resource requirements meet and plans are fully vetted and analyzed."[35]

A second, but similar proposition is to create a standing Joint Command, ready to deploy with assigned and apportioned forces to perform the stability and reconstruction mission and associated building partnership capacity mission. This command would be

---

[33] U.S. Special Operations Command, *Factbook 2012* (2012), 22.
http://www.fas.org/irp/agency/dod/socom/factbook-2012.pdf (accessed April 13, 2012).
[34] Jeffrey E. Marshall, Brig Gen, ARNG (Ret), *Skin in the Game: Partnership in Establishing and Maintaining Global Security and Stability* (Washington, DC: National Defense University Press, 2011), 45.
[35] Ibid., 31.

called the Stability and Reconstruction Joint Command (S&R JCOM) and would deploy

to fill the gap between combat operations and long-term development programs.[36]

A disadvantage of this level of organizational change is that it simply calls for

additional coordination at the GCC without substantially changing the way forces are

provided. While it may solve the problem of increased coordination for a whole of

government approach to the problem; it does not solve the problem of lack of specialized

forces for the building partnership capacity mission.

Civil Affairs Command

Another option would be to create a Functional Unified Command called Civil

Affairs Command or Security Cooperation, Stability and Reconstruction Command. As

General Anthony Zinni, USMC (Ret) has suggested, a Civil Affairs Command would

better prepare the U.S. military to conduct these types of operations, because if the other

Departments of the U.S. Government are unable to perform them, then we'd better be

prepared to do so.[37]

In the same way USSOCOM was established to protect the Special Operations

Forces from Service reprioritization of funding, manpower, and equipment, a Civil

Affairs Command protects building partnership capacity forces from withering on the

budget prioritization vine.

Each of the above proposals seeks to address the two main problems with the

current execution of the building partnership capacity mission: the lack of effective

interagency coordination and the requirement for specialized building partnership

---

[36] Hans Binnendijk and Stuart E. Johnson, *Transforming for Stabilization and Reconstruction Operations* (Washington, DC: National University Press, 2004), 53-55.

[37] General Anthony Zinni, presentation to Joint Advanced Warfighting School, (Joint Forces Staff College, Norfolk, VA, February 3, 2012), cited with permission of General Zinni.

capacity forces. None of the above, in isolation, solves both of these problems well while minimizing the organizational change and resultant upheaval. The best solution is to accept a hybrid between increased coordination at the GCC level while requiring the Services to better resource and build the necessary force structure to support the GCC's TCP and Stability Operations needs. As the traditional force provider, the Services should accept some risk to their traditional missions in order to provide the requisite building partnership capacity forces.

CONCLUSION

Throughout the history of the United States of America, there has been an internal debate on interventions into the affairs of other nations. One side of the debate focused on the imperative of exporting security through unilateral, armed interventions to protect the United States from attack while the other focused on building a multilateral approach that worked to prevent conflict. That debate is not over; ever increasing budget pressures on the Department of Defense are again driving funding decisions and strategy.

As the strategic guidance from the *National Security Strategy*, *National Defense Strategy* as represented in the latest *Quadrennial Defense Review*, and the *National Military Strategy* reveal, there is a slight change in emphasis on the need to improve the capacity of partner nations between the civilian leadership and the military leadership. The break between the National Defense and National Military Strategies highlights the division between those in uniform that seek to prepare for the worst case scenario of war with peer or near-peer competitors instead of increasing the capacity of partner nations to provide for their own security. The *2012 New Strategic Defense Guidance* reveals that the military leadership's argument has succeeded. Their call for a flexible and adaptable force that prepares for conventional wartime tasks, but is somehow prepared to switch over to the building partnership capacity mission without adequate training and investment is a flawed strategy based on hope. It does not "address current and emerging security challenges that do not fit into the rigid stove-pipes of the current system, more suited to the geopolitics of the nineteenth century than the global politics of the twenty-first."[1]

As the environment continues to become more complex with state and non-state actors exploiting the asymmetric vulnerabilities of an open and connected United States, threats are likely to keep emerging from the ungoverned regions of the world with potentially devastating consequences. It is time the United States took this threat as seriously as those posed by enemy conventional forces and invested in the training and resources needed to combat this threat. The training required is specialized; language skills and cultural awareness training are a good start. In the case of building partnership capacity, the training may require a year's investment at a minimum and multiple deployments to a region of interest to hone the required skills and relationships necessary to effectively accomplish the building partnership capacity mission.[2]

In addition to the training requirements, resources in terms of number of personnel permanently assigned to the mission and equipment that meets the requirements of partner nations need to be allocated. Light attack aircraft, mobility systems, littoral combat ships, tactical vehicles and small arms and tactics are the necessary equipment for many of the at risk partner nations struggling to secure their borders and provide internal security, but these programs are underfunded to support the purchase of high-end, costly weapons programs such as 11 carriers, the Joint Strike Fighter, and the Army's new tactical vehicle, which are of little value to the partnership

---

[1] M. J. Williams, "The Coming Revolution in Foreign Affairs: Rethinking American National Security," *International Affairs* Vol 84, Issue 6 (October 17, 2008): 1109.
[2] Congressional Research Service, *Building the Capacity of Partner States Through Security Force Assistance, United States Senate, by the Congressional Research Service, May 5, 2011* (Washington, DC: Government Printing Office, 2011), 36.

building mission. As SOF programs have shown, a little investment in highly-skilled teams outfitted with affordable equipment can pay huge dividends in regional security.

The Services, however, are not making this investment. For example, the United States Air Force decided not to fund the additional building partnership capacity personnel in the Contingency Response Groups. In other words, in an organization of over 300,000 personnel, the Air Force decided that it could not allocate less than 100 people solely focused on the partnership building mission, even though dedicated forces to the achievement of this mission is exactly what is required for successful partner capacity building.

Forces that are not trained to perform partner capacity building are not as effective as those with the requisite training and experience. It wastes resources to pull someone out of their operational specialty, send them through minimal training, and then deploy them for building partnership capacity only to return them to their specialty once that deployment is complete. In the end, they perform neither job as well as they could perform either if focused on only one mission set. This out of hide approach is inefficient and ineffective.

The Geographic Combatant Commanders have described their need for building partnership capacity beyond their resources. Additionally, they outlined the need for adept and constant coordination with other U.S. government agencies and departments to coherently and consistently address the problems in their regions. As understanding of the threat from the ungoverned regions of the world continues to take shape along with the realization that killing our way to victory is a dead end on the road to mission success, the demand for organizations and trained personnel that specialize in building partnership capacity will also increase. If the inertia of the individual Armed Services proves too difficult to overcome in providing the required building partner capacity forces to the Combatant Commanders, then alternatives that will better provide a coherent capability from all U.S. government agencies and departments should be explored.

Several options, such as a separate Civil Affairs Command, a national-level Global Security Agency, or an even bigger increase in SOF teams focused on FID and SFA might be considered to pull this responsibility from the Services and provide a single organizational focus. In much the same way that USSOCOM was established to preserve SOF capability from Service pressures, a new organization responsible for the organizing, training and equipping of building partnership capacity forces should be explored.

Building partnership capacity with persistent and well coordinated efforts provides a good return on investment by avoiding costly wars and preparing those dedicated forces for stability operations should wars occur. Investing in this capability for the United States will improve its image as a global leader working to improve the conditions for less fortunate nations. This cannot be understated in its impact for security in the homeland, as violent extremist organizations thrive in the fertile recruiting grounds of lawless, ungoverned spaces and in the minds of men.

As the self-proclaimed global leader, the United States has the obligation to engage globally with partner nations. It is time the Department of Defense took this obligation by design, and not by default.

GLOSSARY[1]

Term	Description
Building Partnership Capacity (BPC)	Targeted efforts to improve the collective capabilities and performance of the Department of Defense and its partners.
Counterinsurgency (COIN)	Comprehensive civilian and military efforts taken to defeat an insurgency and to address any core grievances
Counterterrorism (CT)	Actions taken directly against terrorist networks and indirectly to influence and render global and regional environments inhospitable to terrorist networks.
Direct Support	A mission requiring a force to support another specific force and authorizing it to answer directly to the supported force's request for assistance.
Foreign Internal Defense (FID)	Participation by civilian and military agencies of a government in any of the action programs taken by another government or other designated organization to free and protect its society from subversion, lawlessness, insurgency, terrorism, and other threats to its security.
Foreign Military Financing (FMF)	Congressionally appropriated grants and loans which enable eligible foreign governments to purchase U.S. defense articles, services, and training through either FMS or direct commercial sales.
Foreign Military Sales (FMS)	That portion of United States security assistance authorized by the Foreign Assistance Act of 1961, as amended, and the Arms Export Control Act of 1976, as amended. This assistance differs from the Military Assistance Program and the International Military Education and Training program in that the recipient provides reimbursement for defense articles and services transferred.
General Purpose Forces (GPF)	Conventional (non-special operations) forces organized trained and equipped by the services for meeting the needs of the Combatant Commanders.

---

[1] Congressional Research Service, *Building the Capacity of Partner States Through Security Force Assistance, United States Senate, by the Congressional Research Service, May 5, 2011* (Washington, DC: government Printing Office, 2011), 59-60.

Humanitarian Assistance (HA)	Programs conducted to relieve or reduce the results of natural or manmade disasters or other endemic conditions such as human pain, disease, hunger, or privation that might present a serious threat to life or that can result in great damage to or loss of property. Humanitarian assistance provided by US forces is limited in scope and duration. The assistance provided is designed to supplement or complement the efforts of the host nation civil authorities or agencies that may have the primary responsibility for providing humanitarian assistance.
Indirect Support	Foreign internal defense operations that emphasize the principle of a host nation's self sufficiency.
International Defense And Development (IDAD)	The full range of measures taken by a nation to promote its growth and to protect itself from subversion, lawlessness, insurgency, terrorism, and other threats to its security.
International Military Education and Training (IMET)	Formal or informal instruction provided to foreign military students, units, and forces on a nonreimbursable (grant) basis by offices or employees of the United States, contract technicians, and contractors. Instruction may include correspondence courses; technical, educational, or informational publications; and media of all kinds.
Irregular Warfare (IW)	A violent struggle among state and non-state actors for legitimacy and influence over the relevant population(s). Irregular warfare favors indirect and asymmetric approaches, though it may employ the full range of military and other capacities, in order to erode an adversary's power, influence, and will.
Joint Combined Exchange Training (JCET)	A program conducted overseas to fulfill US forces training requirements and at the same time exchange the sharing of skills between US forces and host nation counterparts. Training activities are designed to improve US and host nation capabilities.
Peacekeeping Operations (PKO)	Military operations undertaken with the consent of all major parties to a dispute, designed to monitor and facilitate implementation of an agreement (cease fire, truce, or other such agreement) and support diplomatic efforts to reach a long-term political settlement.

Security Assistance (SA)	A group of programs authorized by the Foreign Assistance Act of 1961, as amended, and the Arms Export Control Act of 1976, as amended, or other related statutes by which the United States provides defense articles, military training, and other defense related services by grant, loan, credit, or cash sales in furtherance of national policies and objectives.
Security Cooperation (SC)	Activities undertaken by the Department of Defense to encourage and enable international partners to work with the United States to achieve strategic objectives. Includes all DOD interactions with foreign defense and security establishments, including all DOD-administered security assistance programs, that: Build defense and security relationships that promote specific U.S. security interests, including all international armaments cooperation activities and security assistance activities. Develop allied and friendly military capabilities for self-defense and multinational operations. Provide Service members with peacetime and contingency access to host nations.
Security Force Assistance (SFA)	DOD activities that contribute to unified action by the USG to support the development of the capacity and capability of foreign security forces and their supporting institutions.
Security Forces	Duly constituted military, paramilitary, police, and constabulary forces of a government.
Security Sector Reform (SSR)	The set of policies, plans, programs, and activities that a government undertakes to improve the way it provides safety, security, and justice.
Special Operations Forces (SOF)	Those Active and Reserve Component forces of the Military Services designated by the Secretary of Defense and specifically organized, trained, and equipped to conduct and support special operations.

BIBLIOGRAPHY

Ackerman, Spencer. "An Evolving Role for the Army." *The Washington Independent*. October 7, 2008. http://washingtonindependent.com/10768/army (accessed February 19, 2012).

Armstrong, James, Major, USA. *From Theory to Practice: The Powell Doctrine.* Army Command and General Staff College, 2010.

Barnett, Thomas P.M. *The Pentagon's New Map.* New York: Penguin Group, 2004.

Binnendijk, Hans, and Stuart E. Johnson. *Transforming for Stabilization and Reconstruction Operations.* Washington, DC: National University Press, 2004.

Brannen, Kate. "U.S. Defense Bill Limits DoD-State Fund." *DefenseNews.com*. December 13, 2011. http://www.defensenews.com/article/20111213/DEFSECT04/112130311/U-S-Defense-Bill-Limits-DoD-State-Fund (accessed April 13, 2012).

Center for Global Development. *"On the Brink: Weak States and US National Security."* Washington, DC: Center for Global Development, June 8, 2004.

Chairman, U.S. Joint Chiefs of Staff. *The National Military Strategy of the United States of America 2011, Redefining America's Military Leadership.* Washington DC: Joint Chiefs of Staff, February 8, 2011.

Chairman, U.S. Joint Chiefs of Staff. *The National Military Strategy of the United States of America 1997, Shape, Respond, Prepare Now -- A Military Strategy for a New Era.* Washington DC: Joint Chiefs of Staff, 1997. http://www.au.af.mil/au/awc/awcgate/nms/strategy.htm#Elements (accessed February 29, 2012).

CNN. "Senate approves Iraq war resolution" October 11, 2002 CNN. http://articles.cnn.com/2002-10-11/politics/iraq.us_1_biological-weapons-weapons-inspectors-iraq?_s=PM:ALLPOLITICS (accessed February 18, 2012).

Collins, John M. "Special Operations Forces in Peacetime." *Joint Force Quarterly : JFQ* no. 21 1999. http://ezproxy6.ndu.edu/login?url=http://search.proquest.com/docview/203604654?accountid=12686 (accessed February 29, 2012).

Congressional Research Service. *Africa Command: U.S. Strategic Interests and the Role of the U.S. Military in Africa: A Study prepared for Members and Committees of Congress, by the Congressional Research Service*, Ploch, Lauren. April 3, 2010. Washington, DC: Government Printing Office, 2011.

Congressional Research Service. *Building the Capacity of Partner States Through Security Force Assistance: A Study prepared for Members and Committees of Congress, by the Congressional Research Service, May 5, 2011.* Washington, DC: Government Printing Office, 2011.

Congressional Research Service. *U.S. Conventional Forces and Nuclear Deterrence: A China Case Study: A Study Prepared for the U.S. Congress by the Congressional Research Service, August 11, 2006.* Washington, DC: Government Printing Office, 2006.

Congressional Research Service. *Weak and Failing States: Evolving Security Threats and U.S. Policy: A Study Prepared for the U.S. Congress by the Congressional Research Service, August 28, 2008.* Washington, DC: Government Printing Office, 2008.

Daniel, Lisa. American Forces Press Service, "U.S., African Forces Mitigate Terror Group's Impact." under USAFRICOM media links. February 23, 2012. http://www.africom.mil/getArticle.asp?art=7639&lang=0 (accessed February 25, 2012).

Davidson, Janine Anne. *Learning to lift the fog of peace: The United States military in stability and reconstruction operations.* University of South Carolina, 2005.

Eizenstat, Stuart E. and John Edward Porter. "Weak States are a US Security Threat." *The Christian Science Monitor.* Jun 29, 2004. http://ezproxy6.ndu.edu/login?url=http://search.proquest.com/docview/40567823 5?accountid=12686 (accessed February 24, 2012).

Flournoy, Michele A. and Shawn W. Brimley. "Strategic Planning for National Security: The New Project Solarium." *Joint Forces Quarterly* 41, 2nd Quarter (2006): 80-86.

FOX News. "Obama Sends U.S. Troops to Central Africa to Aid Campaign Against Rebel Group." FOX News.com under Politics. October 14, 2011. http://www.foxnews.com/politics/2011/10/14/obama-sends-us-troops-to-central-africa-to-aid-campaign-against-rebel-group/ (accessed February 25, 2012).

Gaddis, John. *Surprise, Security, and the American Experience.* Cambridge, MA: Harvard University Press, 2004.

Galdorisi, George and Dr. Darren Sutton. *Achieving the Global Maritime Partnership: Operational Needs and Technical Realities.* 2007. http://dspace.dsto.defence.gov.au/dspace/bitstream/1947/8669/1/RUSI%2520Paper%2520Final.pdf (accessed February 20, 2012).

Gates, Robert M. "A Balanced Strategy: Reprogramming the Pentagon for New Age." *Foreign Affairs*, vol 88, no 1 (January/February 2009): 28-30.

Gates, Robert M. "Helping Others Defend Themselves." *Foreign Affairs*, vol 89, no. 3 (May 2010): 2-6. *Academic Search Premier*, EBSCO*host* (accessed April 11, 2012).

Gates, Robert M. Speech to the U.S. Global Leadership Campaign, July 15, 2008. http://www.defense.gov/speeches/speech.aspx?speechid=1262 (accessed April 13, 2012).

Gordon, Philip. *Winning the Right War.* New York: Henry Holt and Company, 2007.

Gray, Colin S. *Another Bloody Century: Future Warfare.* London: Wiedenfeld and Nicholson, 2005.

Gray, Colin S. *Hard Power and Soft Power: The Utility of Military Force as an Instrument of Policy in the 21st Century.* Carlisle, PA: Strategic Studies Institute, 2011.

Groover, Ralph, Lt. Col., USA. *United States Special Operations Forces Strategic Employment.* Carlise, PA: U.S. Army War College, May 3, 2004.

Hamm, Carter, General USA, Commander USAFRICOM. *House and Senate Armed Services Committees Testimony before the 112th Congress.* 5 April 2011.

Harris, Seymour E. "Cost of the Marshall Plan to the United States", *The Journal of Finance* , Vol. 3, No. 1 (Feb., 1948) http://www.jstor.org/stable/2975441 (accessed February 26, 2012).

Historical tables: Budget of the United States Government, Fiscal Year 2012. Washington DC: U.S. Government Printing Office, 2012.

Hoehn, Andrew R., Adam Grissom, David A. Ochmanek, David A. Shlapak, and Alan J. Vick. *A New Division of Labor: Meeting America's Security Challenges Beyond Iraq.* Santa Monica, CA: RAND Corporation, 2007.

Hoven, Randall. "Iraq: The War that Broke Us—Not" *AmericanThinker.com.* August 22, 2010. http://www.americanthinker.com/2010/08/iraq_the_war_that_broke_us_not.html (accessed February 26, 2012).

Klausner, Konrad. *Can Air Mobility Command Meet New Building Partnershp Capacity Objectives?* Carlisle, PA: U.S. Army War College, March 24, 2011.

Lydon, Mike. "'Right Tech' Solutions for USAF Security Force Assistance'. *Small Wars Journal.* September 29, 2010.

Mahan, A. T. *The Influence of Sea Power Upon History, 1660-1773.* New York: Dover Publishing, Inc., 1987.

Marquis, Jefferson, et al. *Developing an Army Strategy for Building Partner Capacity for Stability Operations.* Santa Monica, CA: RAND Corporation, 2010.

Marshall, Jeffrey E., Brig Gen, ARNG (Ret). *Skin in the Game: Partnership in Establishing and Maintaining Global Security and Stability.* Washington, DC: National Defense University Press, 2011.

Messineo, Carol. *The United States Military as an Agent of Development: Counterinsurgency Doctrine and Development Assistance.* The New School: International Affairs Working Paper 2010-05, 2010.

Mills, Nicolaus. *Winning the Peace The Marshall Plan and America's Coming of Age as a Superpower.* Hoboken, NJ: John Wiley and Sons, Inc., 2008.

Mullen, Mike, Admiral, USN. "We can't do it alone," *Honolulu Advertiser*, October 29, 2006. http://the.honoluluadvertiser.com/article/2006/Oct/29/op/FP610290307.html (accessed February 20, 2012).

Musicant, Ivan. *Empire by Default, the Spanish-American War and the Dawn of the American Century.* New York: Henry Holt and company, 1998.

Nugent, Walter. *Habits of Empire: A History of American Expansion.* New York: Vintage Books, 2009.

Nye, Joseph S. *Soft Power: The Means to Success in World Politics.* New York: Public Affairs, 2004.

Pogue, Forrest C. *George C. Marshall: Statesman.* New York: Penguin Books, 1987.

Powell, Colin L. "U.S. Forces: Challenges Ahead," *Foreign Affairs,* (Winter 92, Vol 71, Issue 5) http://tv3wq6ms5q.search.serialssolutions.com/?ctx_ver=Z39.88-2004&ctx_enc=info%3Aofi%2Fenc%3AUTF-8&rfr_id=info:sid/summon.serialssolutions.com&rft_val_fmt=info:ofi/fmt:kev:mtx:journal&rft.genre=article&rft.atitle=U.S.+Forces%3A+Challenges+Ahead&rft.jtitle=Foreign+Affairs&rft.au=Powell%2C+Colin+L&rft.date=1992-12-01&rft.pub=Council+on+Foreign+Relations&rft.issn=0015-7120&rft.volume=71&rft.issue=5&rft.spage=32&rft.epage=45 (accessed February 29, 2012).

Powell, Colin L. "A Strategy of Partnerships," *Foreign Affairs* 83, no. 1 (2004): 22-34, http://ezproxy6.ndu.edu/login?url=http://search.proquest.com/docview/214293195?accountid=12686. (accessed February 29, 2012).

Powell, Colin L. "No Country Left Behind" *Foreign Policy* (January 5, 2005) http://www.foreignpolicy.com/articles/2005/01/05/no_country_left_behind (accessed February 29, 2012).

Rattenbury, J. Freeman. *Remarks on the Cession of the Floridas to the United States of America and the Neccessity of Acquiring the Island of Cuba by Great Britain,* 2nd Ed. (London, 1819), Note: Extracted from the Pamphleteer No. XXIX, For October 1819), 2-5. http://hdl.handle.net/2027/nyp.33433067332746 (accessed February 18, 2012)

Record, Jeffrey. *The Creeping Irrelevance of U.S. Force Planning.* Strategic Studies Institute, 1998.

Roberti, John E., RDML, *Strategic Guidance and Planning,* Presentation to the Joint Forces Staff College, 29 July 2011.

Roosevelt, Franklin, U.S. President *Fourth Inaugral Address,* (1945) http://millercenter.org/scripps/archive/speeches/detail/3337 (accessed February 21, 2012).

Sacolick, Bennet S. "Persistent Engagement: Why Foreign Internal Defense is Important." *Special Warfare* 24, no. 3 (2011): 43 http://ezproxy6.ndu.edu/login?url=http://search.proquest.com/docview/915871222?accountid=12686 (accessed February 29, 2012).

Stavridis, James, Admiral, USN, Commander USEUCOM. *House and Senate Armed Services Committees Testimony before the 112th Congress.* 2011.

Stiglitz, Josesp E. and Linda J. Bilmes. *The Three Trillion Dollar War: The True Cost of the Iraq Conflict.* New York: W.W. Norton and Company, 2008.

Sweeny, Patrick C. *A Primer for: Guidance for the Employment of the Force (GEF), Joint Strategic Capabilities Plan (JSCP), the Adaptive Planning and Execution (APEX) System, and Global Force Management (GFM).* The United States Naval War College Joint Military Operations Department, 29 July 2011.

Teichert, E. John. "The Building Partner Capacity Imperative." *DISAM Journal of International Security Assistance Management* 31.2 (August 2009): 116-125. http://search.proquest.com/docview/197766575/abstract?accountid=12686 (accessed April 12, 2012).

"United States: Togetherness in Libya; Lexington." *The Economist* (April 02, 2011): 30. http://ezproxy6.ndu.edu/login?url=http://search.proquest.com/docview/85977189 5?accountid=12686 (accessed April 13, 2012).

U.S. Africa Command Combined Joint Task Force-Horn of Africa. "2012 Fact Sheet." http://www.hoa.africom.mil/pdfFiles/Fact%20Sheet.pdf (accessed February 25, 2012).

U.S. Department of the Air Force. *Institutionalizing Building Partnerships into Contingency Response Force.* Washington DC: Department of the Air Force, April 2010.

U.S. Department of the Air Force. *2011 Air Force Global Partnership Strategy.* Washington DC: Department of the Air Force, 2011.

U.S. Department of the Air Force. *AFDD 3-24: Irregular Warfare.* Incorporating Change 1, July 28, 2011. Washington DC: Department of the Air Force, 1 August 2007.

U.S. Department of the Army. *Stability Operations,* United States Army Field Manual No. 3-07. Washington DC: HQ Department of the Army, October 6. 2008.

U.S. Department of the Army. *2011 Army Strategic Planning Guidance.* Washington DC: HQ Department of the Army, March 25, 2011.

U.S. Department of the Army. *The U.S. Army Concept for Building Partner Capacity, 2016-2028.* TRADOC Pamphlet 525-8-4. Washington DC: HQ Department of the Army, 22 November 2011.

U.S. Department of Defense. *DoD Directive 3000.05: Stability Operations.* Washington DC: Department of Defense 16 September 2009.

U.S. Department of Defense. *QDR Execution Roadmap Building Partnership Capacity.* Washington DC: Department of Defense, 22 May 2006.

U.S. Department of Defense. *Quadrennial Defense Review Report*. Washington DC: Department of Defense, 1 February 2010.

U.S. Department of Defense. *Quadrennial Defense Review Report*. Washington DC: Department of Defense, 6 February 2006.

U. S. Department of Defense. *Training Requirements for U.S. Ground Forces Deploying in Support of Operation Iraqi Freedom*. Inspector General Report No. D-2008-078. Washington DC: Department of Defense, 9 April 2008.

U.S. Department of the Navy. *A Cooperative Strategy for 21st Century Seapower*. Washington DC: Department of the Navy, October, 2011.

U.S. Department of the Navy. *Naval Operations Concept 2010, Implementing the Maritime Strategy*. Washington DC: Department of the Navy, 2010.

U.S. Department of State. *Quadrennial Diplomacy and Development Review—Leading Through Civilian Power*. Washington DC: Government Printing Office, 2010.

U.S. Department of State, "Our Work," Bureau of Conflict and Stabilization Operations, http://www.state.gov/j/cso/ourwork/index.htm (accessed April 12, 2012).

U.S. Joint Chiefs of Staff. *Department of Defense Dictionary of Military and Associated Terms, Joint Publication 1-02, As Amended through 15 January 2012*. Washington DC: Joint Chiefs of Staff, 8 November 2010.

U.S. Joint Chiefs of Staff. *Special Operations*. Washington DC: Joint Chiefs of Staff, April 18, 2011.

U.S. Joint Chiefs of Staff. *National Military Strategy*. Washington, DC: Government Printing Office, February 2011.

U.S. President. *Sustaining U.S. Global Leadership: Priorities for the 21st Century Defense*. Washington DC: Government Printing Office, January 2012.

U.S. President. *National Security Strategy*. Washington DC: Government Printing Office, May 2010.

U.S. President, *National Security Strategy*. Washington DC: Government Printing Office, September, 2002.

Vick, Alan J. et al. *Air Power in the New Counterinsurgency Era: The Strategic Importance of USAF Advisory and Assistance Teams*. Santa Monica, CA: RAND Corporation, 2006.

Watson, Ken. "Implementing an Integrated Approach to Train SOF for the FID Mission." *2011 JSOU and NDIA SO/LIC Division Essays*. JSOU Report 11-4, July 2011.

Weinstein, Jeremy M., John Edward Porter and Stuart E. Eizenstat. "On the Brink: Weak States and US National Security." Washington, DC: Center for Global Development, June 8, 2004.

Williams, M. J. "The Coming Revolution in Foreign Affairs: Rethinking American National Security." *International Affairs* Vol 84, Issue 6 (October 17, 2008): 1109-29.

Wilson, Woodrow, U.S. President. *War Addresses of Woodrow Wilson* (with an Introduction and Notes by author Roy Leonard) Boston: Ginn and company, 1918.

Wuestner, Scott G. *Building Partner Capacity/Security Force Assistance: A New Structural Paradigm.* Carlisle, PA: The Strategic Studies Institute, February 2009.

Yerex, Derek. "Changing Approaches to Economic Reconstruction: Lessons Learned and Not." Dalhousie University. Canada, 2009. http://ezproxy6.ndu.edu/login?url=http://search.proquest.com/docview/30506701 7?accountid=12686. (accessed February 26, 2012)

www.ingramcontent.com/pod-product-compliance
Lightning Source LLC
Chambersburg PA
CBHW081844280526
45789CB00007B/2564